THE
GIFT
OF
PERSPECTIVE

Wisdom I Gained from
Losing a Leg and Two Lungs

LINDSEY ROY

Figure.1
Vancouver / Toronto / Berkeley

23 24 25 26 27   5 4 3 2 1

Cataloguing data is available from Library and Archives Canada
ISBN 978-1-77327-186-6 (hbk.)
ISBN 978-1-77327-187-3 (ebook)
ISBN 978-1-77327-188-0 (pdf)

Design by Teresa Bubela
Cover illustration adapted from Pacha M Vector | stock.adobe.com
Author photographs by Stefanie Werths

Editing by Steve Cameron
Copy editing by Melissa Churchill
Proofreading by Alison Strobel

Printed and bound in Canada by Friesens
Distributed internationally by Publishers Group West

Figure 1 Publishing Inc.
Vancouver BC Canada
www.figure1publishing.com

Figure 1 Publishing works in the traditional, unceded territory of the xʷməθkʷəy̓əm
(Musqueam), Skwx̱wú7mesh (Squamish), and səlilwətaɬ (Tsleil-Waututh) peoples.

To Aaron, Mitchell, and Morgan.

~~~

To my organ donor and family.

CONTENTS

Prologue

FROM THE TIME the boat hit me to the moment they gave me anesthesia in the operating room, I kept wondering, *Am I going to die?*

I asked my husband and friends on repeat, "Do you think I'm going to die?" I bet I asked it 50 times in five minutes. I was met with various responses—all empathetic in the "you're going to be okay" zone.

The EMT who joined me in the back of the ambulance on the way to the emergency helicopter was also the recipient of this question. I distinctly remember our exchange:

Me: "Do you think I'm going to die?"

Him: "You know, I'm really not sure."

What? Not sure! Maybe just give me your best poker face in that moment? As I came to find out, my call was on his very first shift ever as a volunteer EMT. Poor guy! The helicopter pilot (an awesome female pilot who looked like a badass coworker of mine) and the helicopter nurse also got to hear me ask that question about 20 times on our 30-minute sunset flight.

"Hey, do you think I'm going to die?"

So, the next morning when I woke up in a postsurgical anesthesia fog with an intubation tube down my throat, my first thought was, *I didn't die!*

When the medical team and my husband informed me that my leg had to be amputated the night before to save my life, it barely registered with me. All I could think was, *I'm alive. I didn't die. I can handle the rest.* Everyone who cared for me was shocked and alarmed at my new fate, but I was lifted up by a greater perspective. "I am alive!"

That initial perspective sustained me for a couple of days, but then reality started creeping in one little slice at a time. I couldn't even roll over in my bed without help. I had to have two people slide me down a special wooden board to a portable toilet after my catheter was removed. One week earlier I was an independent mother of two and a corporate executive, and now I was getting a sponge bath from a stranger. The bloom was off the rose of "I am alive."

But somewhere in these moments of missing half a leg and part of another—and seeing even the simplest daily tasks as challenges—I began to unwrap the life-changing gift of perspective.

Introduction

WE ALL HAVE STORIES. Life, as it turns out, happens to each of us. I believe it is powerful to tell our stories because, when we share, others may learn from the paths we have uniquely traveled. And each time we tell our stories, we add to our collective wisdom, creating more empathy and understanding as we go. Ultimately, storytelling reminds us that we are all in this together.

Collected in these pages is my story, or rather, stories. Plus, the stories of others who have inspired me along the way. My sincere hope is that in sharing these stories and the insights contained within, you will find inspiration to help you navigate whatever life has brought your way.

After all, perspective, like the radio, is free. All you need to do is choose which station you're going to tune in to.

THE ACCIDENT

You never really think about the color of the bottom of a boat until you find yourself trapped underneath one.

It was August 10, 2013.

It was the Saturday of a long-weekend lake getaway that had been planned months in advance. Five couples in all left a collective 11 kids behind with grandparents and other willing helpers. We arrived on Thursday and unpacked the coolers and meal supplies, ready for a weekend of adult R&R. We all lived in Kansas City and the lake was in Arkansas, four hours away from home. Lake weekends are common in the Midwest as we obviously don't have access to oceanfront beaches, but we have plenty of heat and humidity in the summertime and need to cool off.

My husband, Aaron, and I had done this same trip a few times before. Our good friends owned a boat and organized these vacations, this time inviting some different couples from various circles of their lives. This would be a time to get to know some new friends and enjoy a relaxing weekend.

No one could have predicted what the 10 of us would go through together that weekend.

The first full day of lake activity was typical. Some sunned on the dock; others took turns going out on the boat. Aaron, though very athletic, is not much for water sports. I, on the other hand, had a little experience waterskiing, so I participated when it was my turn. That first day out on the water, Aaron took several photos and videos of me skiing and tubing. (In hindsight,

I sometimes wonder if he knew something deep down in the part of himself beyond logical comprehension.)

The last time I went out that day was the best I'd ever skied. I didn't want to let go; it felt so invigorating. The sun was starting to set over the water, and I felt strong and invincible as I mastered the ebbs and flows offered by the boat wake. It was a magical feeling.

Saturday began much like Friday had. Everyone headed down to the dock inside our little cove for what we anticipated was going to be a perfect day. Sparkling, clear lake water in this large rock-bottomed lake. The sky was blue and the sun was out. The temperature was perfect. No plans. No to-do list. No worries.

One of the couples had brought this gigantic eight-seater floatie aptly branded the Relaxation Station. We were going to spend the day chilling in the water with this little inflatable island. We decided to swim it out farther into the lake to fully enjoy the clear water and the warm sun and avoid the inevitable dock slime. To make sure the Relaxation Station didn't veer too far away, we used the boat anchor to hold it in place.

When it was time to pack up, I realized the anchor holding the giant floatie in place had snagged on the rocky bottom. It was impossible for me to pull it free by myself. My friend, the boat owner, threw on her life jacket and swam out to help. We tugged and tugged, but to no avail. So we signaled for her husband to come pull up the anchor with the boat.

To make way for the boat, we swam several yards away. In no time the anchor was successfully retrieved, and the boat was parked back in the slip. My friend and I then attempted to swim the floatie back to the dock for the evening.

To this day I'm not exactly sure what happened next, but over the years I've pieced together enough different vantage points of the event to be able to tell the story. After the boat was parked, another boat came buzzing by the "no wake zone" of our cove. This created waves that caused our boat to bash against the side of the dock. In an effort to protect the boat, the driver (who was always a very responsible boat captain) decided to back it up. My friend and I were unaware of this at that moment, and something went awry with the speed and trajectory of the boat. It came directly at us.

I didn't see it coming. I was instantly sucked under the boat by the propeller. I remember feeling trapped and in complete disbelief about what was happening. I also remember noticing the bottom of the boat was white.

I don't know how long I was under there before the engine kill switch was pulled. It was likely only seconds, but it felt like 20 minutes. This well-known phenomenon is how our brains work when under extreme duress, especially in accidents. Time seems to slow down. I recall my brain playing a repeat track of *I can't believe this is happening* over and over. And then I remember a moment of mental silence. It was very much like the "clear the mechanism" scene from the movie *For the Love of the Game*, where Kevin Costner's character drowns out all distractions and focuses only on the pitch he needs to throw. In that moment of silence, I thought about my kids: Mitchell, our son, who was four at the time, and Morgan, our two-year-old daughter. My distinct and clear thought was that I was not going to leave my kids without a mother.

The water was probably 50 feet deep. Since I had been sitting in a giant floatie, I wasn't wearing a life jacket. The irony is that if I had been wearing a life jacket, I probably would have died as it would have been harder to escape from under the boat. I have no idea, though, how I managed to swim out with one working limb. I can remember every detail of that day, even all the moments in the minutes and hours after, but I cannot remember swimming out. I believe God was there, guiding me through.

As everyone on the dock, including my husband, desperately searched for me, I finally popped up in the water, yelling, "Help! Help me!" I distinctly remember how crazy it was that I still had my sunglasses on.

After I was helped to the dock and laid out next to the boat that had mangled me, I looked once at my injuries and was absolutely shocked at the sight of my body. I decided I couldn't look again, so I stayed focused on the beautiful view of the blue sky and puffy white clouds. Chaos ensued around me as my husband ran to get his belt to use as a makeshift tourniquet. Cell reception was poor at the lake, so a friend knocked on a neighbor's door and asked to use their land line to call 911. I continued to ask the friends gathered around me, holding my body together, "Do you think I'm going to die?" I'm not sure how many times I asked that, but I know it was a lot.

Volunteer paramedics showed up, put me on a stretcher, and ran me up the hill to a waiting ambulance. I was driven to a field where an air ambulance helicopter was waiting. There was only room on the helicopter for me, the pilot, and a nurse, so Aaron had to watch me fly away, unsure of what was going to happen. I was transported to Springfield, Missouri, to the closest hospital with the necessary trauma resources.

I remember seeing the sun starting to set for the evening as the helicopter landed on the hospital helipad. I'm sure I disrupted a lot of lives that Saturday evening; there were so many medical professionals running around when they wheeled me into the emergency operating room. Questions were being thrown at me, and I did my best to answer. "Can you move this?" "Do you feel this?" The last thing I recall from that evening is a pair of giant scissors cutting my brand-new swimsuit. And then blackness.

The next morning I woke up with a tube down my throat and my husband and parents in the room. They took the tube out and informed me my left leg had been amputated to save my life. My right leg was severely injured, but the doctors were trying to salvage it. And my right arm had also sustained injuries.

That Sunday, instead of driving home to pick up our kids and get ready for another week of life as planned, our new reality was me lying uncomfortably in a hospital bed in Missouri, hours away from home. "Don't worry," I said that first morning, with a bit of levity to break the tension, "I'll write a book and become a professional speaker and only have to work one day a month." I had no idea what I was in for.

I spent the next year learning to walk again and struggling through so many mental and physical challenges. The years that followed were full of ongoing adaptation as well as an unfolding sense of purpose gleaned from this crazy life experience.

It took me eight years to finally feel ready to "write the book," and I was fairly far along with the manuscript when another lightning bolt struck.

THE DOUBLE LUNG TRANSPLANT

I didn't have COVID-19 and had never been a smoker. But my lungs were destroyed.

Clearly, I had faced hardship before, but I had accepted my leg loss and was living a normal life again. I felt like a grateful over-comer, someone who had lived through an extreme challenge and survived. I had run the proverbial marathon and got the T-shirt. So, to find out I had been thrown back to the starting line again— more like 20 miles behind the starting line—was devastating.

In the fall of 2021, I began experiencing extreme shortness of breath, especially with any exertion, even from something minor like walking up a flight of stairs. I didn't have COVID and was otherwise healthy. It was a mystery no one could solve. I had visited a handful of doctors over the course of a few weeks and continued to hear that all my tests looked normal. Finally, after a very challenging Saturday night, with my shortness of breath causing my heart to race, I called a friend of mine who is a cardiologist. He immediately made room for me in his schedule and performed a couple of major tests on my lungs and heart. Long story short, I was diagnosed with a rare condition called pulmonary arterial hypertension caused by an autoimmune disease (systemic scleroderma, also known as limited scleroderma or CREST syndrome). Basically, the blood vessels in my lungs were constricted, putting major stress on my lungs and heart. The right (pulmonary) side of my heart was under enormous pressure and as a result was three times too big. (I was the opposite of the Grinch.)

This diagnosis felt like another boat I didn't see coming. The condition does not have a permanent fix, meaning for the rest of my life, 24-7, I would have to carry a pump attached to a line in my chest that administered tiny nanograms of medicine that could dilate the blood vessels in my lungs. I would never again be without this pump. I would sleep with it. Shower with it. Carry it everywhere. And it wasn't small—about the length of a brick and about half as thick. It also required a special medicine formula that we had to mix at home every 48 hours using a sterile multistep process.

I couldn't believe I had another rare condition that required another contraption to manage. At least with my prosthetic leg I could take it off now and again. It was certainly a part of me. But this pump! This pump and the medicine it fed my body was a literal lifeline. Like it or not, me and the pump, we were together forever.

As you can imagine, having a new permanent sidekick is challenging. It was extra difficult for me. I already had a sidekick, and after eight years we were kicking butt! Adding a new teammate to the mix was frustrating to say the least. It was also confusing because I was so grateful a therapy like this existed to help me breathe again and eventually save my life, but it was incredibly life-altering at the same time. I lived in constant fear the pump would fall off the bed or out of the pack I carried it in and yank the line out of my heart. Sometimes it would malfunction, causing the alarm to sound at the most inopportune times—like while I was driving or presenting in front of a few hundred people. And when it stopped pumping, the race was on to troubleshoot the issue as my body was reliant on that medicine.

Come springtime, just when I was starting to adapt and feel hopeful that I was on the path to normalcy again, it became clear my new lifetime pal wasn't working out as my medical team hoped it would. I was still short of breath, and my heart was still under duress.

So, bigger pump? Stronger meds? Nope. Double. Lung. Transplant.

Hearing my doctor speak these words was like getting run over by a boat. (I should know.) Total and absolute shock. Why me? Why this? Why now?

My condition was deteriorating rapidly, and I couldn't breathe sufficiently on my own. So, yet another member joined the team—my portable oxygen machine. It was like I was the embodiment of the Fantastic Four—team Keep Lindsey Alive! But my body needed many more liters of oxygen than the portable machine could muster, so on to the old-school large green oxygen tanks we went. We hauled those tanks everywhere because I had to have oxygen 24-7 or my body would freak out. At home I had an oxygen-generating machine, which was easier than the tanks but had its own set of challenges. I had a 50-foot tube hooked to my nasal cannula that allowed me to walk around the house while tethered to the oxygen. I would get the tubing caught on just about everything, and my family had to constantly step over it.

I was put on the lung transplant list on June 13, 2022, and miraculously received my double lung transplant less than a month later on July 7. The next three months were spent going to the hospital every day like it was my job, after spending two and a half weeks, including some very crazy days, as an inpatient. Those months consisted of blood tests, X-rays, pulmonary rehab, clinic visits, IV therapy, all the things. Not to mention trying to be a good mom through it all, with my kids now in middle school.

At the end of September, I "graduated" from the first phase and went home. As I write this, I am eight months post-transplant.

One unique and extremely challenging part of my transplant story is I wasn't allowed any food or water by mouth for several months following the transplant. That's right—zero to eat or drink through my mouth. Not even an ice chip. It might not sound like much, but pause for a moment and really think about it. You don't realize how much of the world you experience through your mouth until you can't. The reason I couldn't have *anything* orally was because my underlying autoimmune disease had also affected the function of my esophagus. As a precaution, I was put on a feeding tube for my nutrients and water. The concern was that my compromised esophagus might cause food or water to come back up, where it could be aspirated into my new lungs and make them sick. This is not typical for lung transplant recipients—it was only due to my specific condition. I continued to discover I am a medical unicorn. This is still something I am figuring out and managing.

During this incredibly challenging time, I was forced to take my own advice from my leg journey. The book I was writing when

I became sick with my autoimmune disease was now also my guidebook for getting through an unimaginably hard time. Life was imitating art.

So, you are not alone, dear reader. If this book finds you feeling all hope is lost, know that I have been there too. Multiple times. And I have found joy again.

And if you are reading this book without a major crisis on your hands, there will be something in here for you as well. I have found time and time again that applying the insights gathered in these pages makes it easier to handle almost any challenge.

This book does not delve deeply into new research or provide checklists or formulas. It is a compilation of insights forged in fire, both by me and by those I've met along the way. It is a book straight from the trenches, wrapped in mud and dust and hopefully a bit of humor too. It is a book that encourages you to take power in controlling what you can about any predicament—your perspective—and harnessing that for the greater good of yourself and others. It's a book that can meet you where you are and be applied to work, health, parenting, and life in general.

I'm humbled to have you join me on this journey and encourage you to share your story too. We can all learn from each other.

We all have a perspective. Here's mine.

We can complain because
rose bushes have thorns
or rejoice because
thorn bushes have roses.

ANONYMOUS

CHAPTER ONE

Choose Your View

Sustain the Power of Perspective

EXACTLY ONE YEAR after I lost my leg, we took a family vacation to the beach. Maybe it was a strange choice to return
to any sort of body of water on the anniversary of the most
terrifying moment of my life, but we had discussed this trip pre-
accident and it became a goal of mine to make it happen. Plus, no
boats were on the itinerary! So, there we were, slathered in sunscreen and armed with towels, kids' floaties, and sand toys. There
were lots of other families there. I'm sure many of the moms were
thinking things I might ordinarily have been thinking: *Seriously,*
could this swimsuit be any more horrible? Could I be any fatter
or pastier? Do the kids have on enough sunscreen?

I know all those feelings well. On the morning of my accident,
a near-supermodel friend was taking a photo of my husband and
me and I was thinking I looked absolutely terrible in my bathing
suit. I had no idea that was the most perfect my body would ever
be for the rest of my life.

Now here I was on this beach trip a year later, and I'll tell you, my concerns were very different. The main thing on my mind was the waterproof foot I was carrying in my beach bag. My normal prosthetic foot is a wonder of technology. It can sense terrain and mimic human ankle movement. But that requires electronics. I literally charge this foot every night the same way I do my cell phone. Because my foot is not waterproof, I need a separate foot for the beach. So, after we picked our spot on the sand, I took foot B out of my bag and changed out foot A with an Allen wrench.

As I sat there in that surreal moment, most of me was just happy to be there. It was a temporary high. As the day went on, negativity took over. My leg was hurting. This waterproof foot was literally a piece of wood carved to look like a foot—tricky enough to walk on, let alone traverse a football field full of sand or play with my kids. By the time we got back to the hotel, I hobbled into the room in pain, ready to bawl my eyes out. I couldn't stop thinking about what that same trip would have been like with two fully functioning legs and feet. I couldn't stop thinking about the other people at the beach and their working legs and feet. I locked myself in the bathroom to shower. Standing there, I willed myself into a new perspective. I literally said, out loud, things like:

"I am lucky to even be here."

"So many people can't travel for so many different reasons."

"If anyone had told me six months ago I'd walk on a beach today, I would have been elated."

"With this waterproof foot, I'm standing up in the shower for the first time in a year. It feels . . . fantastic."

This isn't just Pollyanna stuff. After a few minutes of this type of thinking, I started to see the situation differently. The mere process of forcing myself to flip my thinking changed my entire outlook. My energy was flowing down a different road. I could feel it.

And what did it take? It didn't cost me any money. I didn't have to take a pill. I created my own little chemical reaction in my brain by using the free and abundant resource of a broader perspective. By making myself pause and actively seek out a new vantage point, I enabled myself to feel so much better.

We all know this feeling. It's the same feeling we get when we hear about something tragic, whether it be on the news or in our community. In these moments we typically say, "Wow, that puts things in perspective." The hard thing we heard trivializes whatever else we were worried about. It instantly resets our perspective. The problem with this type of perspective shifting, however, is that it is *passive* and reliant on hearing bad news about other people. I've found, through *active* and intentional actions, we can reset our view just like I did in the shower that day. The feeling is the same, it's just as helpful, and it's possible to sustain it.

Studies have proven that the psychological phenomenon behind perspective shifting, positive thinking, not only shifts your emotional state but also leads to better health and possibly better life decisions and a sustained focus on long-term goals.

In the hardest chapters of my recoveries, I invented and practiced ways to shift my perspective, usually out of sheer desperation. To do this, I frequently—obsessively—ask myself a series of questions. Here are a few examples of the questions I asked myself after the accident:

- *How could this situation have been worse?*

The boat could have hit my head or vital organs. It's amazing that it didn't! My kids could have been at the lake that weekend. Thankfully, they weren't.

When you're struggling, ask yourself this question and see if you can think of five ways the situation could be worse. I find I usually only get to two or three before I start to gain some perspective.

- **What is going right?**

I never had any infections in any of my wounds after the boating accident. This alone is a miracle when you consider my mangled body was swimming in lake water. I had good health insurance, so medical bills were not a major stressor. I had a caring support network in every aspect of my life, which was a huge gift.

- **What's the upside in this seemingly terrible situation?**

I won't lie. Many days I struggled to find a good answer to this question. When I lost my leg, I was a mother of a two-year-old and a four-year-old. I was used to my independence and taking care of others, but now, suddenly, I couldn't do one single thing by myself. My career was put on hold. But some days I'd find an answer I could make myself believe:

Perhaps I am meant to use this experience to help others facing hard challenges in life?

Maybe my kids will be more empathetic or independent than average?

A couple of experiences I can remember vividly from early on: Once when I was learning to walk again, my son seemed to intuitively know what I needed to hear. Walking on a prosthesis was new, and it was frustrating and humbling. He looked at me and said, "Hey, Mom, you just walked up that hill really fast." My little two-year-old daughter once came downstairs with a single leg warmer on, telling me, "This is my prosthetic leg, Mama." These memories still bring me to tears.

The biggest thing I learned about this question was that it didn't matter if I discovered an upside. Simply, the practice of regularly asking the question changed my viewpoint.

- ***What have I accomplished today?***

When in the throes of both my major life events, charting the progress I'd made that day, even if it was just a minor milestone, was a key survival tactic.

I still have the neon-green and pink posterboards I wrote my baby steps on during that dark first year after dancing with the propeller. Looking back on those lists, I can see that sometimes the accomplishments were shockingly simple. "Put in my own ponytail today," reads one. "Rolled over in bed," reads another.

Even though these might sound like trivial things, they were everything to me when life was at its absolute worst. Along with my legs, my right arm was badly injured in the accident. Putting in a ponytail was a *huge* accomplishment. Similarly, rolling over was a massive breakthrough.

When I change my perspective to look through this lens, it helps me realize I am making progress. It was also important to try as hard as I could to not compare my current life to my former one, to not focus on what I had lost or *thought* I had lost. Even with my prosthetic leg, I've been able to hike mountains and travel the world.

At first, with my new lungs, walking a few steps was a challenge. But, with intentionality and focus, I have learned not to compare myself to past Lindsey. The powerful effect of looking forward with hope and determination is like starting a flywheel turning. Your small wins build on each other and add momentum, until eventually the process becomes automatic and self-perpetuating. Seeing improvements in my lung capacity, though small from day to day, helped me visualize an upward trend, which was especially useful on the bad days. Recording these little milestones can also provide motivation. I wanted to write down a bigger number every time, and that would make me push myself a bit harder on the rehab treadmill every day. Now, current Lindsey can look back on post-op Lindsey and smile at how far she has come and get excited for what future Lindsey will do.

Simply pausing and thinking about what you have accomplished is a small but incredibly meaningful way to find an upward trend line when you feel you're at the lowest possible point.

~~~

WHEN I WAS IN the first phases of my amputation journey, I really hated to be called an amputee. It felt like a strange club I didn't want to be in. It was all so new to me, and I hated the notion of instantly being labeled by my injuries. I was a human. A wife. A mom. A businessperson. A friend. A sister. A daughter. (And a fan of good food and cold beer.) But suddenly, I was short-handed to "amputee." Plus, I was trying to protect myself from negativity and was scared to talk to others in fear of hearing the hard stuff. I had no desire to attend support groups. I tried a couple of Facebook group pages and read some posts here and there that made me want to cry my eyes out. "My leg is always in pain . . . how am I going to survive?" one read. No thanks, Facebook page. When I was trying like mad to remain hopeful and optimistic, words like this were scarring. I didn't personally know anyone who was an amputee, so I needed someone to look to for both practical and inspirational help, but I struggled to find an answer that worked for me.

And then Amy Purdy waltzed into my life.

A friend sent me a TEDx Talk Amy delivered (TEDx is a regional version of a TED Talk), and it was *everything* to me. Amy, if you don't know her, became a double amputee at the age of 19 after contracting bacterial meningitis and almost dying of sepsis. She was given only a 2 percent chance of living! In her 2011 talk, I saw this healthy and vibrant young woman walking effortlessly around the stage with two prosthetic legs. It was beyond my wildest dreams in those first months. That she was also a world champion para-snowboarder blew my mind. I'd be thrilled just to walk to the mailbox!

I saw a photo of her in the early days after her accident, and she looked just like I had: big bulky prosthetic legs sitting beside the bed, lying there in a depressed mess, surrounded by the distress of the situation and the endless supplies needed in the early days of dealing with such injuries. Seeing her "before" photo and then how she looked on the TEDx stage—her "after"—gave me the courage to think that maybe, just maybe, I could make it to the other side too.

Then, as if through divine intervention, in the winter of 2014, when I still couldn't walk, Amy was a contestant on *Dancing with the Stars*!

By this point I had racked up numerous views of her TEDx Talk along with any other content of her I could get my hands on. And now she was going to be coming to my living room every Monday night. I nearly passed out the first time I saw a commercial featuring her for the upcoming show. Amy's performance, week after week, was a lifeline for me. Seeing her dance with her two artificial legs brought me to tears of hope and inspiration. It allowed me to believe I, too, could live an amazing life much bigger than the confines of my current circumstances.

I've come to call what I did with Amy "borrowing perspective." And once you realize you're doing it, you'll see that you

can borrow perspective from almost any situation or circumstance. In fact, you might not even realize you're doing it—that's
how common it is. But by naming it, and actively acknowledging
when you engage in this behavior, you can boost the efficacy of
your shift in perspective.

As an example, after the first time my kids were allowed to visit
me in the hospital following my amputation, I was especially sad
that night when they went home and I was alone. I was having a
pity party for myself and felt the first big wave of despair following
the initial shock of the accident. I had finally fallen asleep despite
the pain and constant beeps and hospital cords when I was
woken up at 2 AM to go get X-rays. I thought it was complete
craziness that I was getting X-rays in the middle of the night, but
I guess that's when inpatients are scheduled during busy days
(and as I would discover several times over, there is no real dis-
tinction between night and day in a hospital). Those 2 AM X-rays
ended up being just what I needed.

On the way back to my room, the transportation employee
who was pushing my bed and I were talking, and I asked about
her family. My kids were all I could think of that night, so it was
a natural question to ask her on our long walk back. She casu-
ally and without complaint told me she had four amazing kids
but didn't get to spend as much time with them as she wanted
because she was working two jobs. Man, that was dose one of
perspective that night. I was so sad about not spending one night
under the same roof as my kids and this was her life many nights
every week. Then the real kicker—we took a route past the pedi-
atric cancer area of the hospital. I can see that sign in my mind's
eye like it was yesterday. I started to think about how incredibly
tough it would be to see your child sick like that.

People often say, "It could always be worse." That's a bit of a
downer phrase. And while it has resonated for centuries, I prefer

to think of my borrowed perspective as a gift. I'm sure the eight other adults who were spending the weekend with us on the lake also felt similarly. The night that followed and the days after that were probably ones of heightened perspective for them— the gratitude they likely felt for their able bodies borrowed from my accident.

There is no shame in this kind of borrowing. It is a tool to help see the good and to be mindful of what we are taking for granted. Taking a moment to pull up to a wider view gives you a chance to see the countless things in your life that are *not* broken. This kind of perspective is out there for the taking, but you must be willing to look beyond the vacuum of your current view.

When I was first in the pulmonary rehab program after I got my new lungs, I borrowed perspective by watching a guy named Charlie. Charlie is a retired high school principal from Arkansas and a gem of a human. He was in my rehab class and was about six weeks ahead of me on the recovery road. When I watched him on the treadmill, it looked like he was flying. He didn't know it at the time, but watching him on that treadmill was so motivating for me. We became friends in class, and we keep in touch now as we travel this similar road. Later, unbeknownst to me, I was that person to a lung transplant recipient named Wendy who joined rehab after me. On my "graduation day" she gave me a card with the most amazing note about how I had inspired her from afar and helped motivate her. She also made me a beautiful bracelet. Seeing other people walk the road a few miles ahead can give us perspective on a path we can't yet see but desperately want to.

As for Amy, I had the chance to meet her in person at a women's leadership event where she was the closing keynote speaker. A friend of mine was in charge of the event and contacted me immediately when Amy was booked. I tried hard not to fangirl on her too much, but I wanted her to know the hope she lent me by having the courage to embrace vulnerability and tell her story to the world.

When we put our stories out there, we feed this chain of letting others borrow our perspective. I think that's pretty powerful.

~~~

SHIRENE IS A FRIEND I met in pulmonary rehab. Soft-spoken and enduringly positive, at 25 years old she was an internal medicine resident, donning her first white coat in 2021. One of her first rotations was during a later peak of COVID-19, where she cared for patients struggling to breathe. Just days before she finished this rotation to move to the ICU, Shirene found herself short of breath.

Over Thanksgiving break she checked herself into the hospital. She had lost her senses of taste and smell, and that escalated to nausea, vomiting, low blood pressure, and a high fever. Her lungs were in major distress, and very quickly she saw herself in the same shoes as her COVID-19 patients, though she tested negative for the virus during her entire hospital stay.

Shirene wrote an article about her experience for a University of Missouri–Kansas City magazine. Here is her harrowing story:

> The couple months that followed [my hospital admission] were a blur, as I was intubated, placed in a medically-induced coma, and transferred to another hospital for ECMO (a heart-lung machine), as my lungs continued to fail. My family had to make the hard decision of placing me on the lung transplant list on December 21, 2021. After waiting about a month and a half, I received my double lung transplant in February of 2022, which came with its own complications, including hemorrhaging

requiring almost 50 units of blood, a liver hematoma, a pulmonary embolism, and kidney failure requiring dialysis. However,
the hardest part was yet to come.

The most important part of life post-transplant is rehabilitation of the new lungs. I was placed on a special floor that focused
on weaning [patients] off their ventilator, physical therapy,
occupational therapy, speech therapy, and respiratory therapy.
The hardest part of these by far was weaning off the vent. When
you have experienced the feeling of hypoxia [low blood-oxygen
levels] and the feeling of asphyxiation, you become reliant on
the thing that can prevent that. My recovery took a step back
just shortly after my birthday when my dad passed away from
Stage IV lung cancer. With the encouragement of family, friends,
and the staff, I came off the ventilator (and feeding tube) a
month later and was finally able to communicate verbally and
eat solid food. About a month after that, I was discharged home
to continue outpatient rehab.

Those six months in the hospital, while one of the most
challenging times in my life, was also the most life-changing,
not only in personal life, but also my professional life. I have a
greater sense of what it means to be a patient, sitting alone in
your bed, seeing only one to two visitors a day, being disturbed
throughout the night for blood draws, waking up at 6:45 AM
for physical therapy, and having only those despicable green
swabs for water. The best memories I had were ones where the
care was focused on what would be best for me, from the staff
pushing me to the park or the helipad while on a ventilator,
feeding tube, and continuous IVs; [to] the secretary melting
down an orange popsicle so I could swab it on my birthday;
[to] the night nurse and tech sitting by me when my father
passed away. Those were the moments I cherish most. When
I'm back at the hospital rounding on my patients, I hope to put

my white coat over my patient gown and focus on what matters most: patient-centered care.

Shirene has metaphorically "walked a mile in someone else's shoes." She now has hard-earned perspective that will make her the kind of doctor who really cares about her patients. This kind of empathy means everything from the patient's point of view. Shirene is going to do big things in this world, and I can't wait to watch.

However, while we can't all walk a mile in someone else's shoes—nor would we necessarily want to—we can be intentional about how we gain perspective and come closer to understanding things from other points of view.

In 2017, I was privileged to be invited to give my own TEDX Talk. I wanted to provide hope and inspiration to others, to put my story out there for someone else to hopefully borrow perspective from. My talk, "What Trauma Taught Me About Happiness," was part of a larger series named "Where You Stand Matters." There is a heck of a lot of meaning packed into that notion, especially for me. The other speakers at the event had many unique perspectives, ranging from how bees use an incredibly sophisticated collective wisdom to make decisions for the hive to the best way to experience a solar eclipse (which was a big thing in 2017—remember those glasses?).

This idea of where you stand matters is an eloquent way to say perspective is simply how you see things. It reminds me of the experience we've all had of hanging a picture on the wall. If you try to hang something by yourself, you are inevitably too close to it to hang it straight. That's why we either have someone else at a distance tell us to inch it up or down to help us get it right or we purposefully change our vantage point and run back 10 feet to see what we need to adjust.

This recognition that we can be too close to something to see it clearly is important. It's why organizations have a board of directors. It's why we need people in our lives who can give us honest feedback. It's why constructive criticism can be a gift. It's why we need others to tell us they believe in us when we don't believe in ourselves. It is also why we should seek out meaningful conversations with people who may see the world differently. Seeing the other side of an argument is a critical skill.

After all, reasonable people can disagree. We all know smart and respectable people who think about topics differently than we do. Politics. Vaccines. Parenting styles. Music. Mullets.

Despite this truth, people today struggle to relate to others who hold opposing points of view. There are many theories about the increasing divisiveness in today's world, but I think it's a commonly held truth that people are more divided now, in many ways, than in previous generations. Maybe it's the effect social media algorithms have on our confirmation bias. Or maybe it's the fragmented and siloed way we consume news today, compared to past decades when most of the country got its news from a single source (think Walter Cronkite). Whatever it is, I think the onus is on us to purposefully seek out different vantage points—to change where we stand—and to try to see the validity of the other side of an argument.

It was fascinating for me to watch my husband serve on the school board during the COVID-19 pandemic. Well-meaning people with very different viewpoints on in-person versus virtual learning or required versus optional masking or any other related topic tended to think their viewpoint was the majority viewpoint. That happens because we—consciously or unconsciously—look for evidence to validate our own perspective. In complex situations (which this was), there are typically very valid points on both sides of a debate.

This notion of changing where you stand to consider an alternate point of view matters because it's another skill in the power of perspective toolbox. This doesn't mean you have to agree or change your mind, of course, but when you can at least understand where someone is coming from, it can help lessen the divide. When you know and respect someone with a different viewpoint, it creates a degree of empathy for and acceptance of opposing views.

The practice of seeing from multiple viewpoints also helps you to consider various ways of solving any problem you may be facing. Part of the autoimmune condition that eventually caused my lung issues showed up a decade earlier, via super cold hands and fingers. It's called Raynaud's syndrome, and many people (especially women) suffer from it. For most, it's just an annoyance where your fingers may turn white or blue and feel super cold. For me, my fingers would sometimes get skin ulcers that were more painful than some of my surgeries. I would constantly hold a warm cup of tea at work. My team even gifted me a pair of USB-powered, heated computer gloves.

This is a common symptom of my autoimmune condition in the milder cases, which is what I had for several years. Despite it being common, it was painful. I was desperate to find a remedy, so I got outside of my comfort zone. I tried Botox in my hands. That was very uncomfortable and didn't work. I explored a cream used for people with a completely different condition. Nothing. You know what worked the best to rid me of this extreme pain? Chiropractic care. I explored that along with acupuncture and sure enough, chiropractic adjustments every once in a while made my fingers dramatically better. If I didn't go for an extended period of time, they would get worse again.

It takes intention to seek out additional perspectives and tap into the ideas of people who stand in different places.

For your work, it could mean doing 360-degree feedback where you solicit perspectives from your coworkers or team either formally or informally.

At home, it could mean asking your family what they think you are doing well and where they wish you would adjust. Every once in a while, I tell my kids and husband we are going to do family performance reviews. Each person gets to tell the other members of the family one thing they really appreciate and one thing they wish the other person would start/stop/change. It's fascinating to hear what rises to the top, and if you are open to the process, it can offer some pretty interesting insights. This is also something I do with my kids one on one. My son is now a teenager, and I've found it helpful to give him this kind of moment where he can freely give me feedback. Like most kids, he gets plenty of feedback from his parents, so it's useful to turn the tables. The feedback he has given me has been key in keeping our relationship and our lines of communication strong.

I like to think of these different perspective feedback loops as inputs. Not every one of them will lead to action; not every one of them will be good. We each must make our own choices about what to listen to and what to ignore. However, having the opportunity to see if your proverbial picture is hanging on the wall perfectly level or six inches off is a powerful use of perspective.

~~~

MICK EBELING IS one of those captivating and energetic speakers who has an incredible story to tell. He is also the type of guy who seems to effortlessly ooze coolness—tall and skater-looking with his flat-brimmed hat and Chuck Taylors. He even has a kid named Angus.

Several years ago, I had the opportunity to hear Mick speak. He is the founder of an organization called Not Impossible Labs. They love to ask absurd questions and then try to solve them for the good of humanity. They focus their work by asking, "Can improving one life change the course of humanity? We believe the answer is yes." They consider one person's challenge and look for a way to take a wrong and make it right, with the idea being that by improving one person's life, the resulting solutions may spur innovation and spark further ideas.

Some Not Impossible Labs projects take months, and others years. The thing that connects them all is using tech to push the boundaries of what is thought possible. "Don's Voice" is one of the stories I've heard from Mick and his team.

Don and Lorraine Moir ran a family farm in Lucan, Ontario, when Don was diagnosed with amyotrophic lateral sclerosis (ALS) in 1995. Fitted with a ventilator in 1999, Don lost his ability to speak. Lorraine heard Mick talking about another project, the eye-writer, on the radio and got in touch with Not Impossible Labs to ask if they could create a digital solution to help Don communicate.

Not Impossible Labs jumped at the chance and found a way to give Don his voice back. The team accomplished this by utilizing a combination of hardware, insight, and software from SpeakYourMind Foundation to develop a simple interface that uses eye-tracking technology to allow Don to communicate. Through this technology, Don was able to independently write a love letter to his wife and audibly say "I love you, Lorraine" for the first time in decades. Sadly, Don died from complications of his disease in 2019.

Another impossible made not impossible circumstance that Mick and his team tackled was centered on Daniel Omar. Daniel was 14 when he lost both of his arms in a bombing raid on his village in South Sudan.

The absurdity that Mick and Not Impossible Labs saw was that more than 50,000 people in South Sudan had lost limbs due to ongoing conflicts and had no reliable access to prosthetics. Inspired by Daniel's story, in 2013, the team found a way to covertly enter the country and set up one of the first—if not the first—3D-printing prosthetic labs and training facilities in the world. Through the lens of Daniel's challenge, people in the village learned how to replicate the process and create custom 3D-printed limbs for others. Daniel got two new arms and was able to feed himself for the first time in two years.

"It only seems impossible until it's done" is a timeless phrase that is a core tenet of the power of perspective and the human ability to keep pushing against expectation, to disrupt, to innovate, to overcome. It is the underlying ethos that Mick's company is founded on, and it's also a reason I'm alive today.

When I was first diagnosed with pulmonary hypertension, I was told about an innovator named Martine Rothblatt. Martine's daughter was diagnosed with the same condition at age six. The family first noticed she was having trouble keeping pace on a family vacation, then she started struggling to get on the school bus due to shortness of breath.

Martine was a founder of Sirius Radio, a pioneer of the satellite radio world. When she learned of her daughter's condition and prognosis—essentially five years to live—Martine shifted boldly to a new calling: to save her daughter. She exited Sirius and used all her time and resources to find a way to save her daughter's life, despite many medical and pharma professionals telling her it wasn't likely.

Martine, driven by the greatest purpose of saving her child's life, defied the odds. She founded a pharmaceutical company called United Therapeutics and bought a molecule formulation that eventually yielded a new drug that could dilate those challenged blood vessels via a constant infusion of the medicine through a permanent port. Her daughter is now in her thirties, thanks to this invention.

This was the very same medicine I was prescribed that was administered via the pump that was always with me. While my condition didn't adequately respond to this medicine, the solution Martine created slowed the decline of my lungs, buying me precious time to get the gift of a lifetime with my new lungs.

Martine is currently spearheading research and solutions for lung transplants. One of the exploratory directions involves personalized pigs, an idea that has been documented in *Bloomberg* and other publications. Pigs are ideal animals for this because their organs are roughly the same size as humans' and they have relatively short gestation periods. Harvesting pig organs has the potential to increase the desperately needed supply of available organs. The real innovation is the personalization part. The current thinking is a pig can be altered with a specific person's DNA, which could ensure the person's body doesn't reject the transplanted organ. Who knows where this will go, but make no mistake, Martine is changing the world. I'm sure grateful she's out there pushing for what's next.

Whether it's to solve the rare challenges you've been given, like Martine, or to be inspired to solve other people's challenges, like Mick at Not Impossible Labs, harnessing the courage to do things differently is a potent use of your power of perspective. That doesn't mean you have to change the world. Rather, this mindset can help you overcome the hurdles you face daily, from forcing yourself to break bad habits to pushing yourself to try something new even though you are unsure of the outcome. Like everything with perspective, success requires an open mind and intentionality.

⌒

MY "GOOD" LEG is my right one. After my accident, the doctors had to fight hard to keep it from requiring amputation as well. I had lost about six inches of my fibula (the outside lower leg bone) as well as key tendons and muscles.

Despite knowing I was missing a large chunk of my fibula, it shocked me to see it again nearly eight years later when I got an X-ray on that leg while nursing a wound. I had seen an X-ray of it before, but it was in that blurry post-accident phase, so I didn't really remember it. When you look at my leg from the outside, it looks like a shark took a huge bite out of my outer calf. On the inside, via the X-ray, you can see there is a gap where my fibula should be. Above and below the "shark bite," there are remnants of fibula that used to connect and areas where tendons and muscles used to be. Now it's just a big gap. Despite all that, my right leg works really well. It has taken me from the lights of Hong Kong to my hometown's watermelon festival and through all the countless steps of daily living.

It all comes down to my amazing tibia, which bears all of my weight, along with a tendon that was moved around to do its old job plus the job of the tendon that's damaged. The tendon loss was the most debilitating aspect of recovery for my right leg, because I couldn't walk without a clunky leg brace to make my foot work right. So, I decided to have another surgery— a tendon transfer—that would hopefully make things work a little better. My surgeon reattached my remaining leg tendon to the center top of my foot. This "elective" (elective seems relative when you've had a traumatic accident!) surgery did more than make things a little better—it was a huge success! But not immediately.

My brain had believed for over three decades that my inner tendon was used to move my foot inward and downward. But now that same tendon had to do more, to compensate for the missing tendon—and my brain didn't know how to do this yet. So, post-surgery, if I wanted to move my foot up, I had to concentrate and tell my brain, "Move foot in." Over time and lots of foot movement, my brain learned the new pathways.

Reattachment. This is a powerful metaphor when it comes to the power of perspective. My reattached tendon and the new neural pathway I formed awakened in me the idea that it is okay to redirect our hopes and dreams, and even our sense of self.

The morning of my accident, I asked a friend to take a picture of Aaron and me on the dock of our lake house rental. This isn't something I would have normally done, but, as I have reflected on it over time, it seems like there was a lot of foreshadowing that day. That picture became the last photo I have of my able-bodied self, and it was taken in the same bathing suit on the same day everything went down. The same suit that would be cut off me with giant scissors just hours later.

When I posed for that picture, I can remember feeling a little self-conscious to be standing there basically in underwear with a beautiful new friend with a "perfect body" taking our photo. I remember thinking to myself the only way I would post this on social media is with some serious cropping.

Fast-forward to now and I wish I could have been kinder to myself. When I look at that picture today, I don't see my less-than-flat stomach. I don't see round thighs. I see two perfectly functional legs (and lungs). But that reality is gone, replaced by a new reality, one where I've had to set new goals for myself and find new ways to meet other lifelong goals.

We all have strengths and we all have weaknesses. To succeed in this life, we need to find our tibia and lean on it—just like we need to lean on others for support when the going gets tough. This is a reminder to be grateful and to focus on what you do have—what is working, what is going right. We have all been broken in some way before, and that imperfection is what makes us unique, and uniquely beautiful.

In Japan, a millennia-old technique called kintsugi is used to repair broken ceramics. Instead of trying to make the broken object perfect again—as this is impossible—the ceramics are repaired with lacquer and powdered gold. The result is a uniquely beautiful piece that highlights and honors the flaw as something to reveal rather than conceal. It represents a history that cannot be escaped and celebrates it, adding to the beauty of the object.

A lot of people ask questions about my legs, because they are often visible. I don't try to hide them and never sought out a cover to make my prosthetic leg look like a "normal" leg. I go full carbon fiber and metal, as this is who I am now.

This notion of cherishing the flaw as its own unique and beautiful addition became even more salient for me after my lung surgery.

It goes without saying that having a double lung transplant is major surgery. And with major surgery comes scars. I have a long scar line across my chest that looks like the underwire of a bra (it's called a clamshell incision). I have scars on my abdomen that are remnants of where plastic tubes drained my chest cavity for days after the surgery. You can still spot the site where the medicine pump used to be inserted into my veins. I have a hole above my belly button where my feeding tube goes into my body. If my feeding tube ever permanently comes out, I will have yet another scar. These scars hide well enough under my shirt, but they are forever a part of me. When I look at them today, I don't think of them as *scars*; they are my kintsugi, and the beautiful thing they reveal is the gift of life I was given by an organ donor and his family. My scars are a validation of my existence. Their beauty translates into my continued perseverance.

We may be broken, but through the power of perspective, we can see that we are beautiful.

WRAP-UP

Of everything I have learned through my journey, perspective is at the top of the list. It is the most powerful and most untapped resource we have to heal, hope, and even to innovate. Perspective is powerful and completely within our control.

One day you will tell your story
of how you overcame what
you went through and it will be
someone else's survival guide.

BRENÉ BROWN

CHAPTER TWO

Open Up

Explore Vulnerability

I SPOKE AT A Forbes conference for chief marketing officers a few years ago. The other speakers had great tales of new branding campaigns, innovative product launches, and explorations of modern marketing capabilities. I have had the privilege of working at Hallmark Cards, one of the best marketing companies that has ever existed, for the past 23 years. At over a hundred years old, the brand remains in the highest tier in brand studies every single year. So, there were many stories I could have told that group of peers. However, I decided to tell a personal story.

While preparing for the conference and discussing some of the key themes with the conference organizers and other speakers, the concept of authenticity kept coming up. This notion of authenticity rings especially true in marketing and advertising. The days of campaigns that use sleight of hand or fun characters and jingles—the likes of which *Mad Men* highlighted

39

for us all—are over. Marketing has become so much more complex. People don't want to be sold to or pushed. They want to find products and services that work for them. Many want to know what's in the products they buy, where they were made, and who made them. They want to have a conversation with a brand and feel proud to be part of the brand "family."

Take the Dove beauty company, for example. In 2013, they produced the *Dove Real Beauty Sketches* short film, as part of a larger ad campaign, in which women were asked to describe themselves for an FBI forensic artist to sketch. Next, a stranger was asked to describe the same woman while the artist sketched. The artist had never seen the women—he could only go by what he was told. The women and the artist then viewed the two resulting sketches together, and the self-described portraits were always seen as less pleasing and less accurate than the stranger-described portraits.

This famous campaign highlighted notions of self-acceptance, authenticity, and vulnerability, and it generated a tremendous response. Within a year, this campaign, and others like it, nearly doubled the profits of the company.

The dot I tried to connect through my talk that day, while using my accident story as the vehicle, is that vulnerability is the key to unlocking authenticity. In the Dove campaign, this is illustrated by the women who displayed vulnerability in sharing their true thoughts about their appearance. As a result, the reality (or authenticity) of how women tend to perceive themselves less generously than strangers came to light.

As a further example of this relationship between vulnerability and authenticity, here's a little excerpt of what I shared at the Forbes conference that day:

The story I want to tell begins a few years ago. I lived what most would describe as a normal life. I was married with two kids and was an emerging leader at Hallmark, working my way up the corporate ladder. I was doing little things, like playing with my kids in the sand, not thinking twice about it.

At work, I was developing my leadership brand. I was a hard worker. A team player. I was always authentic, never pretending to be somebody I wasn't. But there was something I wasn't. I wasn't vulnerable. I wanted to be the A student. And vulnerability is a key part of authenticity.

After all, I was still developing my leadership brand, and therefore, I believed it to be in my best interest to not allow myself to be too vulnerable. I bought in to the conventional wisdom indicating that we should be very cautious about sharing too much of ourselves at work. I believed in order to be taken seriously and to get my ideas heard, I needed to be guarded and fit into my own perception of what a successful, professional woman looked like. I wanted to be measured, in control, and independent. To not show weakness. To have all the answers.

Here is an example of how that manifested for me: Around that time, my communications manager was leading the work to try and bring an authentic leader voice to our employee communications. So, we started an employee blog on our intranet featuring posts from leaders across the company, including me. Blogs were fairly new at the time, and it was a good idea to explore internally.

I observed as several of my peers were creating posts that blended authentic moments from their lives into work lessons to great success. My reluctance, however, to show that side of myself meant that this is the type of content I went with. The title of my post was "How Do You Spell Benign Saboteur?" This terminology was from a recent corporate training session. It didn't scream "must read." To be fair, there was nothing wrong with the post, or the topic, at all. But it certainly didn't get nearly the buzz of that of my peers. I'm not kidding when I say my views were terrible. I was ranked last. I was basically fired as a volunteer intranet blogger.

And then my normal life, and everything I knew about it, changed . . . Suddenly. Dramatically.

I then went on to tell this group of senior executives the story of my accident. I showed these polished professionals pictures of me in a hospital bed next to a portable toilet. I shared some of what I had learned, including the power of being real when I didn't have the fortitude to consider any other option. I shared a bit of authentic writing from my CaringBridge site post-accident versus my guarded blog approach pre-accident. (CaringBridge is a social communications network where those on a health journey can post to their followers, which are made up of the friends and family that you'd typically be sending email and text updates to.)

As I began the incredibly long road to recovery, which included developing new routines for myself and my family, I began to write. My initial aspirations were purely functional: I wrote to keep my friends, family, and colleagues aware of my progress. I wrote to stay connected to my life when it felt like everything else was disconnected from it. As I wrote, I began to receive positive affirmation about what I was sharing—my authenticity and my vulnerability. People even started to share my story with folks I didn't know. I had 30,000 views in a matter of weeks. And it kept growing.

So, I kept sharing. Moments of happiness and accomplishment as well as moments of true struggle. I shared my stories, warts and all, partly because I had an obligation to keep my dear friends and family in the loop but also because it was cathartic to be so honest and real about what I was feeling and experiencing.

Along the way, I found myself not even thinking twice about showing candor and raw honesty in my CaringBridge blog posts, the way I would have in my writing before the accident. I found myself completely committed to turning the accident into something good. I wanted to take my experience and harness it to inspire others and to inspire the work I do. And I got to test it when I went back to work.

Returning to work was no easy feat. I was catching up on what I'd missed, navigating the ridiculously long Hallmark hallways on my new leg, all while still adjusting to my new life. Fortunately, I was lifted up by the colleagues who had followed along with my accident and recovery.

The vulnerability I'd shown as I shared my story on Caring-Bridge made my colleagues feel invested in my progress, and they supported me to a degree I never expected. Their support made my transition easier. And I realized I was okay stepping beyond being vulnerable through a computer screen to being vulnerable in real life.

As I got back into the swing of things with work, I found myself inspired and ready to tackle my work with a commitment to retain the vulnerability and authenticity I had been sharing during my accident recovery. I shared my story in *O Magazine*, *Fast Company*, *Forbes*, *Working Mother*, and at many conferences. There are so many ties between life and work that we all experience, and my freshly formed insights were inspiring the work I was doing. People seemed interested in my story; everyone gets tired of the typical corporate slideshows.

When I did my TEDx Talk, I invited my entire team to attend, in addition to my family and friends.

One of the things I've done to bring that authenticity and vulnerability out to a larger group of employees is something I call "Connect with Lindsey" sessions. Once a month, I bring together a cross-functional group of people. It's truly a mix of job levels, titles, and tenures—about 10 to 12 of us at one time. I spend an hour with that group doing exactly as the title suggests—connecting—by pulling questions from a fishbowl (and/or posted in the virtual chat) and having everyone take turns answering them. Some of the questions are more light-hearted: What was your first job? What's your favorite childhood memory? Others are more business focused: Where do you seek inspiration for your work? If you ran the company, what's the first decision you'd make? I also participate in answering the questions, and we all leave having seen a side of our coworkers that we maybe hadn't seen before. It also has the by-product of reinforcing our brand mission, which is all about connection and caring.

This hour tends to be one of my favorite work hours each month. Undoubtedly, I get to know the people on my team on a deeper level, but I'm also truly inspired by what's discussed, especially given the nature of our business.

And while this was not the intent, the sessions got good feedback, and as a result I received some of the highest employee engagement scores after we began doing these sessions.

At the Forbes conference, what I left those executives with at the end of my talk was this: "What I have found is that vulnerability is key to true authenticity. Sharing and hearing each other's stories gives us new lenses into life, into the emotions we are all trying to tap into. We are all aspiring to represent brands in an authentic way. Maybe that needs to start with us."

Being vulnerable happens when you trust completely. But I've found the reverse is also true. When you're vulnerable, it can establish instant trust. Every brand wants their customer's trust. And in a world where we are constantly seeking authentic connection, it is about time we create space for vulnerability.

As it relates to leadership, I find the best, most successful leaders (in business or life) tend to be the ones who demonstrate personal accountability and do a great job owning the results of their team in the most raw and authentic way when things don't go as planned. This takes courage and a fearless mindset, but it is incredibly helpful. It shows vulnerability, which creates an environment of trust and authentic interactions. That is essential for highly functioning groups of any size and in any arena.

When someone chooses to face reality head-on and shares when a plan or path they have advocated isn't working despite good planning and effort, others will want to be a part of the solution. The work then becomes teamwork, garnering the best insights and solution options from all. The conversation shifts from probing and poking to helping and building. This kind of realism can also lead to making quicker decisions, which can often save invaluable time. Courageous and vulnerable leadership also inspires others to engage more. Instead of sitting back and waiting on one person to deliver the results alone, others are more primed to be active participants on the journey and help carry the load.

Leaders who demonstrate these behaviors (I now count myself in this club thanks to great mentors) increase their credibility. No one wants to think results are being sugar-coated or amended for their consumption. People at all levels, at least the good ones, want the full picture. When you deliver the full picture, along with other signs of credibility—like potential action plans—people aren't looking to find the hole in your argument. They start looking to help *fill the hole* in your problem.

And in work and in life, as best-selling author Brené Brown says, "we don't have to do all of it alone. We were never meant to."

⌁⌁

"WE ALL HAVE STORIES. Life, as it turns out, happens to each of us. I believe it is powerful to tell our stories because, when we share, others may learn from the paths we have uniquely traveled. And each time we tell our stories, we add to our collective wisdom, creating more empathy and understanding as we go. Ultimately, storytelling reminds us that we are all in this together."

This is how I started the introduction to this book. I repeat it here because a key aspect of storytelling—of creating more empathy and understanding—is the authentic display of vulnerability.

And this is precisely the mission of a media company called 8 Billion Ones (formerly called 7 Billion Ones, before, you know, the world's population hit that massive milestone). The organization's calling is to share the written stories of as many "Ones" as possible. Founded by photographer Randy Bacon, the company pairs stories with striking portrait photography, motion portraits, and conversation videos. As director Mandy Vela writes on the splash page of the website, it's all "in the name of shining a light on our most vulnerable pieces, and courageously sharing the experiences that make us both uniquely singular and help us to find the common ground with one another and within our own lives."

Part of my writing journey before penning this book was when I was invited to share my story on the 8 Billion Ones platform. When asked if I knew of others who might be willing to share their story, I thought of a college friend, Kelly, her family, and her son Ryan.

Although Kelly and I didn't know each other well in college, we had mutual friends and we've had some memorable times together. My most vivid memory of her in our younger years was one night when she let me cut her hair on a whim. We had all just graduated, and Kelly had a year of teaching at an elementary school under her belt. She had stopped over at a house I was sharing with another college friend as we were getting ready to go out for the night. Kelly was sporting overalls and an eyebrow ring, along with her cute and carefree smile. She said she needed her hair cut and I offered to do it, even though I had zero experience and didn't even have the right kind of scissors. But she didn't care, and I was overconfident, so we proceeded. I hacked away at her hair, and we went out on the town. She recently told me it was one of the best haircuts she's ever had (which is hard to believe!).

Not long after that night, Kelly got married to a wonderful guy she had dated in college—coincidentally, also named Aaron—and not too long after that they were expecting their first child.

I knew that their son Ryan had complications from birth, and I learned afterward that he was diagnosed with something called Peters plus syndrome. At the time, there were fewer than 50 known cases around the world. Ryan is legally blind and deaf. He can walk, but not well—he's had two knee replacement surgeries. Ryan is nonverbal, but like many people who can't speak, he is perfectly communicative.

I wasn't in their inner circle and didn't recognize that Kelly and Aaron were silently coping with these struggles behind closed doors. "He was 16 and people didn't know much beyond the headlines," Kelly told me. "I could have counted on one hand the number of people who actually knew the detail of what was going on."

Kelly has now shared two stories on 8 Billion Ones. In them she talks of Ryan's initial diagnosis and the anger, fear, worry, and grief she felt. She speaks of the long car rides that are calming for Ryan and shares incredible stories about Ryan's intellect and amazing intuition about people. She shares the difficulties of having to manage Ryan's emotional swings and reminds us to find joy in the little moments.

One of the most touching parts of Kelly's second story are the photos of Ryan wearing a life jacket while bobbing in the ocean waves. He has a huge smile on his face, and you can tell he feels happy and free.

When Kelly was approached about sharing her family's story with 8 Billion Ones, it was a giant pause moment. Deep down, she saw this as an opportunity to put it all out there and change the trajectory her family was on, but there was a lot to consider. What did Aaron think? We all know people process struggles differently. What would be the impact on the two younger siblings who had been added to their beautiful family (a boy and a girl, just a few years younger than Ryan)? She and Aaron agreed they had to do it. It was time.

"I couldn't figure out what to say. One night I cried and prayed, and it all poured out of me. And that was the release, telling the raw story. We didn't tell anyone before we published it."

Freedom ensued. "I felt this release when it got published. Literally all the weight lifted off my shoulders. Physically, I could feel it. It was the most amazing feeling. I didn't have fear anymore. Thank God! It was so freeing to not hide it anymore. I had no idea it could feel so good.

"Sharing our story saved me."

I have witnessed an amazing transformation in Kelly since telling her family's story. She now boldly and courageously shares day-in-the-life photos and stories of caring for Ryan. These posts give so many of us a window into how to understand, how to help, how to advocate, how to care better. Kelly shares stories of how Ryan sometimes scratches and bites her when he gets overwhelmed and stories of the challenges of changing his diaper in a public environment that doesn't cater to those in Ryan's situation. She shares photos of him sleeping in the living room on a mattress on the floor while she sleeps on the couch near him in case he has a seizure and beautiful photos of Ryan during the joyful moments. The most tear-wrenching post is a video of Ryan walking with a classmate across the stage to a standing ovation and thunderous applause when he graduated from high school.

The despair and seclusion Kelly and her family felt when they were putting on a brave face and struggling alone to raise Ryan has been replaced by an outpouring of support and empathy. By choosing to be vulnerable, Kelly and her family have dramatically changed the emotional course of their lives.

For herself, Kelly has become a huge advocate for kids with special needs, pushing for reform at the community and political levels.

Kelly has learned some amazing things from choosing to display vulnerability; I'd like to share a few:

- ***Don't be afraid of showing the ugly.***

Kelly told me that in the very beginning they didn't tell anyone because they were just trying to get by. Eat. Go to work. Take care of Ryan. They were in survival mode. I know many of us can relate to that notion. Now, though, she says,

> I should have talked to people. He had so much going on. It was so hard and ugly and my feelings about it were ugly. I was wrestling with a lot of whys. Then our friends started having babies. That were healthy. So, then it was jealousy. And I didn't think anyone would understand. Part of it was, amidst different times and different circumstances, I felt like I was not the great mom I always thought I would be. Life was so hard

and messy it just seemed so ugly at times. It was so ugly I just couldn't share. I didn't want people to think differently of me. *Kelly is kind, and upbeat, and caring.* That's how I think people saw me. But I was not being those things in my house.

I relate to Kelly on a lot of these points. I'm sure many parents do. When you love so much, it can also make you hard on yourself. I am one of many who can tell you Kelly is a wonderful mom—words can't even describe all she has done and all she continues to do every day. She is full of the biggest love for her family. We could all use a reminder to be as kind to ourselves as we are to others.

During this time, Kelly also didn't want to be seen as angry: "I used to write so many posts in my head but never click Publish. I had anger about what we had to deal with. For instance, I remember going to my younger son's basketball games in the winter. The ramps were all snowed over. I couldn't take Ryan. It made me so angry. I didn't want people to think of me as angry. So, I just stayed quiet."

By being vulnerable, Kelly has found the support she needed to find her voice. And instead of raging out on social media, she's taking action through special-needs advocacy. That is a sterling lesson of channeling your anger and putting it to good use.

- *Know you aren't a burden.*

"I didn't want to be pitied. How could anyone truly understand? If I shared how hard things really were, I was worried people would just feel sorry for us, and we didn't want that on top of everything else."

Kelly didn't want her challenges to be a burden to others—and I can relate completely. So she sucked it up and tried to contain the pain. "I was afraid. I was afraid of my parents seeing me hurting any more than they already were on their own. I was afraid I would make it worse for other people who cared about us. I was afraid I would make it worse if they really knew how hard every day was in our lives."

But, like me, what Kelly found by being vulnerable was a village of people who genuinely wanted to be there to help and take on some of the burden. In her second article on 8 Billion Ones, Kelly wrote about her family's experience taking a beach vacation and sharing lodging with friends and family.

> We were surrounded by our village of people, which made a huge impact . . . because it was also Ryan's village. We were in a house with 20 people that loved us and loved him deeply. Everyone was rooting for us that week. Everyone saw up close how hard even the small things could be [for us] and all our family stepped in to be a help. From taking turns feeding him, taking him for a car ride, helping schlep everything down to the beach, keeping an umbrella over him, bringing snacks . . . there were a lot of extra hands. . . . I could not guarantee this, but I am confident we were covered in prayer by the whole houseful of people daily. Not to mention the love. It was abundant everywhere.

- *Love is out there waiting for you.*

> We were overwhelmed with love [after we shared our story]. So many messages came in that moved us to tears. "I can't believe I didn't know this." Or "I'm so proud of you guys."
>
> Being open and raw gave our friendships a different level of depth. Our family was stunned, thrilled, and proud. Our families shared that post a zillion times. They were proud. I had never

thought about that, I just thought about how they would be hurt to know the level of our suffering. But they were so proud of who we are and what we've been up against.

- ### *Vulnerability begets vulnerability.*

In addition to the love and support the family received regarding their story, Kelly also received many private messages in which others revealed their own struggles to her. This, too, is something that regularly happens to me. Whenever I do a public speaking event, people will often come up to me afterward and share a challenge from their own life. It's amazing how the reciprocity of sharing is so instantaneous and connective. It's like people are just waiting for a moment to share. That's the power of storytelling— it creates more empathy.

As Kelly said, "My vulnerability brought it out in others. So many others who were really hurting with so many things. I was embarrassed that good friends shared things with me that I had no idea about. I have a good friend who had a one-month-old baby that passed away before we met . . . and I never knew she had faced this in her life until we told our story."

Again, I recall receiving similar messages of support after sharing, with authenticity, the struggles I was facing. I've had friends and colleagues tell me about suffering from anxiety (I had no idea) and losing a first husband early in life to a freak situation (again, no idea) and countless other stories of vulnerability, things I didn't know and probably never would have known if I hadn't shared my own authentic story.

We have all heard the quote about being kind to others because you never know what someone else is going through. It's so true—we have no idea in most cases what is going on in someone's life that is causing real struggle. I think we would all be so much better to one another if we had a glimpse into the reality of each other's life. It takes someone to get the ball rolling by being willing to put it all out there and take that scary, yet ultimately freeing, risk of being truly vulnerable.

- **Vulnerability opens paths to purpose.**

As I've mentioned, since sharing her family's story, Kelly has been going full speed ahead into purpose-driven avenues for those with disabilities. In addition to sharing deeply inspiring content with her personal circle, she continues to expand her reach. She found a support and advocacy community with parents of special-needs kids and volunteered to be the lead for Kansas. She helps educate people on how certain votes will impact the disabled community. She shares simple but profound insights born out of her personal struggles. She helps people better understand the Individualized Education Program (IEP) process and how to plan for special-needs care for young adults when school services subside.

And she's only just begun. "I haven't even tapped into what I want to do yet. There's so much opportunity to help. Funding issues. Advocacy issues. Education issues. If you know someone with a disabled child at home, you have to do something once you know. As they say, when you know better, you do better. In the world of disability, you don't know what you don't know. I can say things that people didn't know or understand. You gain momentum once you get this loving response."

I am so proud of Kelly. My overalls-wearing, eyebrow ring–sporting, homemade haircut–having friend, who has logged many days alone in the valley of hardship, has become a free and fierce woman in the world, paving a path for so many others. And what caused this remarkable transformation? Having the courage to be vulnerable. Authentically sharing your own story is one of the most powerful catalysts for change in this world. I urge you to consider allowing yourself to be vulnerable, especially in those darkest of moments we all face.

As a quick sidebar, I want to make this point because I think many people feel like public sharing is "just not my thing." We all know people who can overshare or overdramatize a situation. Whenever I see a post on social media that begins with, "Well, I don't want to start anything here, but . . ." I know it's going to be a drama-causer. I have no space for that in my life.

It's important to understand the difference between being vulnerable and oversharing. It's also important to recognize that this spectrum is unique to each of us.

Timing is a factor. I love what Kelly had to say about this: "Sharing doesn't have to come from the open wound. You may need that survival time first." That is seriously sage advice. Sometimes you need to know a little more about what you are dealing with before you put something out there. There are times when you want to respect the privacy of others. Or maybe you want more concrete solutions before opening up a larger dialogue. In contrast to my leg journey, I waited a full year before sharing my lung journey beyond our inner circle because the situation was continually and rapidly changing.

Audience is a factor too. For some people and some situations, there is an efficiency and a freedom that comes from sharing publicly, on social media or beyond. For other situations, it might be simply writing it down on paper for yourself to give it initial concreteness. Sometimes it might be seeing a therapist or confiding in a friend. In a work setting, it might be sharing with a coworker or your team. Sequencing can also play a role. Perhaps a trial run with a friend first is the perfect stepping-stone to sharing more broadly.

Finally, it's good to consider what outcome you want from sharing. What's your goal? For some, it's about finding help and support. For others, it's about feeling free and authentic. It can also be functional only, like sparing your loved ones from having to answer the same questions about your struggle over and over. (I distinctly remember not wanting my husband to have to repeat my accident story a million times.) Over time, bigger goals like purpose may also be revealed.

When you share and what you share are up to you. If your motivation is genuine, you'll likely find that by sharing, you'll get what you need—and then some.

〜〜〜

WHEN I DECIDED THAT, yes, I would participate in the TEDXKC event, I chose to be more than a little vulnerable.

Sure, I had had some practice opening myself up to the power that comes with displaying authentic vulnerability. I had shared my story on CaringBridge, at work, and to a few other local groups. But those were all caring audiences in safe spaces.

The TEDXKC event required the next level of putting myself out there. Even applying to participate was quite a process; there was a lot of national competition for the 10 available spots at our Kansas City event, which is a big one. I was the only local speaker. The first part of the process required me to partner with the TEDX staff to explore various ways to tell my story. The team was extremely helpful but also full of ideas about which parts of my story were unique and "ideas worth sharing," which is the TED mission. And then I had to consider how a live audience of over 2,000 people would react to my talk.

There is a tremendous quote from Brené Brown that perfectly sums up what it is to be vulnerable in a situation like this:

"I believe that you have to walk through vulnerability to get to courage, therefore . . . embrace the suck." Brown's work in the areas of vulnerability, courage, shame, and empathy (especially as they relate to our relationships) has led to numerous best-selling books (*Daring Greatly: How the Courage to Be Vulnerable Transforms the Way We Live, Love, Parent, and Lead; Dare to Lead;* and *The Gifts of Imperfection*, among many others), a 2010 TEDx Talk that is in the top five most viewed TED Talks ever, and a popular Netflix special.

While there are many quotes from Brown that resonate powerfully with me (and I'll share a couple more), this particular one highlights the process I endured before walking out on that stage in Kansas City. It took vulnerability to pursue the gig (I was turned down the year before). It took vulnerability to prepare my talk in a way that was authentic to my experience while meeting the expectations of the event organizers. And it took courage to walk out on that stage, with legs showing, full metal on one side and the visible "shark bite" on the other. The suck? That was everything in between. The hours of writing and rewriting and memorizing. The moments of reliving the whole ordeal as we searched for new angles and insights. The fear that the audience would find it boring and generic when compared to the other speakers' topics. The panic that I might mess up and have it be captured on film and posted on YouTube to live there forever.

In the end, I'm quite proud of the talk I delivered. It wasn't perfect, but it did receive the only standing ovation of the night, which is another testament to vulnerability. Even though many of the other talks were fabulous, mine was the only one that was highly personal. And as I've said before, if it has helped even one person out of the near 200,000 who have watched it, I will have achieved my goal.

With all that said, I can also fall prey to the pitfalls of vulnerability. Being vulnerable does invite feedback, in big or little ways, depending on how loudly you shout your story.

For me, 99 percent of the feedback I receive is positive and uplifting. However, despite knowing better, humans are conditioned to see and react to the negative instead of the positive, and I was no different after my TEDX Talk. Online, I've had a few thumbs-down votes and negative comments posted. Typical trolling stuff, but it still got to me. I stewed on one comment for a full 24 hours. Eventually I had to take my own medicine and shift my perspective—there were thousands of thumbs-ups and lots of wonderfully positive comments—and refocus.

Again, cue Brené Brown. Her 2012 book, *Daring Greatly*, starts with an excerpt from a speech called "The Man in the Arena" by Theodore Roosevelt. It goes like this:

> It is not the critic who counts; not the man who points out how the strong man stumbles, or where the doer of deeds could have done them better. The credit belongs to the man who is actually in the arena, whose face is marred by dust and sweat and blood; who strives valiantly; who errs, who comes short again and again; who spends himself in a worthy cause; who at the best knows in the end the triumph of high achievement, and who at worst, if he fails, at least fails while daring greatly, so that his place shall never be with those cold and timid souls who neither know victory nor defeat.

My friend Tressa had this quote hanging in her office and shared it with me after I told her about the scarring online trolling. I'd not yet read *Daring Greatly*, and so the words were a breath of fresh air to me. The beauty of Roosevelt's passage is in how eloquently it captures the struggle we all have when we put ourselves out there. To be vulnerable and courageous means going ahead with the well-meaning act knowing there will always be negative people who simply want to judge. And the internet and social media make that all too easy.

As Brown says of those timid souls who neither know victory nor defeat, "If you're not in the arena also getting your ass kicked, I'm not interested in your feedback."

For me, that drove right at the heart of the anguish I was feeling from my first interaction with the inevitable internet trolls. In Brown's 2018 book, *Dare to Lead*, she shares the story of when she first became aware of Roosevelt's passage. It was in 2012, just before she published *Daring Greatly*. She writes, "I found this quote during a particularly challenging time in my career. My TEDxHouston talk on vulnerability was going viral, and while there was a groundswell of support for the talk, many of the criticisms were cruel and personal, confirming my biggest fears about putting myself out there. This was the perfect quote to capture how I felt and my growing resolve to go full-on Tom Petty and not back down."

The message found in Roosevelt's passage has resonated with me and many others. As Brown points out, even LeBron James had "Man in the Arena" written on the side of his basketball sneakers.

But what about the flip side? What about the trolls sitting back and throwing tomatoes into the arena? What about the power of social media to distort reality?

There's an old proverb that says, "It is easier to destroy than it is to create," and the world of internet comment sections is like putting this proverb on steroids. Add to that our predisposition to see the negative and to be self-critical, and all of a sudden the internet becomes a place where it is super easy to tear down others and to tear down ourselves.

First of all, I do believe social media has many positives, and it can be a friend to vulnerability and true connection at times. Communication platforms allow you to broadcast a message to a group of people, enabling efficiency. Kelly used, and continues to use, social media for good, and I used the CaringBridge platform in 2013 in a similar fashion. Social media can also enable you to stay connected—at least in small ways—to people you don't have the opportunity to see in person very often.

More often than not, though, social media is the enemy of vulnerability. (I will also say from my own experience, this isn't always purposeful or conscious, but it's a result of the medium.) For example, social media can distort reality and create idealized content. In September 2021, the *Wall Street Journal* obtained internal Facebook documents detailing the harmful effects of Instagram among a significant portion of its millions of young users, especially teenage girls. A few examples the WSJ shared on these harmful effects:

- "Instagram makes body image issues worse for one in three teenage girls."

- "Teens blame Instagram for increases in the rate of anxiety and depression." The internal study documents this was "unprompted and consistent across all groups."

- "Among teenagers who reported suicidal thoughts, about 6 percent in the US and 13 percent in the UK traced them back to Instagram."

- "The researchers noted that many of these problems are unique to Instagram because it focuses heavily on body and lifestyle, meaning social comparison is worse on Instagram."

I've noticed how social media is often used by young people, especially young women, to share the "perfect picture" to mark nearly every day of their life. I feel like we are at the point in society where too many people are living for what they can post versus just living and maybe posting when something worthy naturally happens.

Family pictures on Facebook or Instagram are another culprit. We want to post the best pictures we take and share our families with others. I'm guilty of this too. Completely! We are proud of our families and should be. And it can feel a little too-much-information-ish or negative to share some family argument or whatever may have went down before the perfect shot was captured. There are plenty of memes out there that poke fun at this situation: Before the photo: "Everybody smile, and I'll give you a treat!" The photo caption on social media: "The reason I breathe." Ha! But it's so true.

As with teens comparing and judging themselves against others, moms and dads are no different. It can be easy from time to time to make comparisons when looking at "ideal" families when yours is facing a challenge, or even just being "normal," meaning not perfect.

Our backgrounds on our video calls are another way we distort our realities and curate our image. When COVID hit and many of us participated in some sort of video calling, people started to think about their backgrounds—especially if it was for work purposes. I did the same. I bought some new art and spruced up a wall in my guest room. One day when I was doing a virtual keynote, I was struck by (and a little embarrassed about) how the background you could see in the video looked organized and well designed while everything out of frame looked like a total disaster.

Trolls are going to do their thing, and other people will post what they post. We can't control how others feel or how they use social media. What we can control is how *we* use it. I don't think we need to necessarily avoid these platforms. I know I'll continue to use Instagram to promote this book, I'll post pics of my kids on Facebook to my private community and truly enjoy looking at the pictures of my friends' families, and I'll spruce up the background before I log on to a video call. I think the thing we all need to remind ourselves of is that others are doing the same. Don't take what you see in the pretty frame as the whole story. Assume there is a deeper side to each piece of content you see. Even if you don't get a window into someone's vulnerable space, remind yourself they likely have one.

And, if and when the time is right, you might consider sharing something on your feed that is less idealized and a little more real. It is a small step toward keeping things balanced and reminding others that there is a sheen to the screen. If you choose to embrace authenticity and vulnerability, my guess is that you'll find it rewarding.

~~~

WHEN I WAS a college senior at Kansas State, we played Purdue in the Alamo Bowl in San Antonio. (Their quarterback that year may be someone you've heard of—a sophomore named Drew Brees.) K-State lost the game in the final minute with an 80-yard drive from the Boilermakers. Heartbreaker. But that's not the point.

The point is that it is incredible that I was even there to see it. While the story I'm about to share might read like two college kids falling into lucky break after lucky break, I like to think of it a little differently now.

The secret message in this story is about the power of relinquishing control. For many, to lose control is to feel naked. To be extremely vulnerable. But sometimes it can be useful to ask yourself, "What is the worst that could possibly happen if I loosen my grip on control?" Often, the results aren't that scary, and if you're lucky like me and my friend Michele were on that beautiful San Antonio night in 1998, you'll open yourself up to possibilities you had not thought possible. This could happen at home, at the office, or anywhere.

On to the story: Michele and I decided to go to the game at the last minute. It was a December 29 game, a perfect little road trip over our holiday break. We didn't have much money, like most college students, and hadn't bought tickets or reserved hotel rooms or any of that jazz. But we assumed we would figure it out. So, we gassed up my *Jetsons*-looking 1989 blue Ford Probe with flip-up lights, a manual transmission, and some leaky sludge coming out of the passenger-side floor vents, and headed south.

Another friend of ours did have a hotel room and offered to let us stay with her, so that major box got checked early into the adventure. As for tickets, we assumed we could score some pre-game on the fun and famed Riverwalk area of San Antonio. But no one, it turns out, was reselling tickets on the Riverwalk. We walked with the crowd to the stadium before game time, thinking there would surely be people barking, "Who needs tickets!" there. No dice.

We walked around the stadium, thinking maybe we'd find someone on the side or in the back with tickets. Crickets. But as we finished our lap, we noticed some kids standing by a side door on the inside of the stadium. We simply knocked on the door, they opened it, and we walked in. Bingo! (I still feel slightly guilty about this . . .) Since we didn't officially have tickets, we weren't sure where to sit. As we pondered this question, we came across a section of amazing seats that were empty-ish compared to the surrounding areas. A sign said it was reserved for the players' family and friends. Well, I was lab partners in my botany class with the K-State QB, so we obviously qualified for these seats, right?

We didn't have cash to buy drinks or snacks, and they didn't take credit cards back then, but somehow a person working behind the beer counter allowed me to write them a check and they gave me cash. (That was a very 1998 sentence!)

The flow didn't stop that night. We decided we were having such a good time we should continue to enjoy our way home and spend a couple of nights in Austin, including New Year's Eve. Clearly, we weren't great at remembering we were broke. We pulled into a random La Quinta Inn off a highway, hoping it would be nice enough and budget-friendly enough for us to afford to spend the night.

While I called my parents from our Motorola "bag phone" (another very 1998 phrase), Michele went to get us a room. As I'm saying good-bye to my fun and understanding parents, I spot Michele walking out with a giant fruit basket and making this "you're not going to believe this" face. She proceeds to tell me the hotel literally just opened its doors and today was their grand opening. We were their very first customers, and they gave us our room (and the fruit basket) for free! They threw confetti and took Michele's picture as their first customer. You can't make this stuff up. The good juju from the trip carried on, and we had so many fun and unexpected things fall in our laps. It was the stuff of legends.

I love that memory. And no, I'm not implying you can stumble haphazardly through life and expect everything to work out. But is there an aspect of your life where you don't really know the answer and want to see where the world might take you?

I've held about 12 different positions in my 23 years at Hallmark, and I've never officially applied for any of them. There's been a lot of variety across those positions as well, ranging from product development to innovation leadership to digital and e-commerce roles to marketing and brand work. I've never plotted out a career trajectory with a specific path or role that I was aiming for. It may be a bit of an unconventional choice, especially to peers I meet in the outside world who have always stayed in their lane, but I have loved the variety that has come my way and the opportunity to learn multiple aspects of the business. Plus, this way of operating has come with the bonus that I've not become obsessed with a predetermined future. I've enjoyed that mental freedom and have allowed myself to be in the moment, fully.

In whatever aspects of your life you give this idea a try, I say, let your heart guide you. Let faith guide you. Let the never-ending dynamism of the world present you with new options. Just don't forget to look and listen. You may just find yourself having the time of your life at the Alamo Bowl.

WRAP-UP

Being vulnerable basically means being exposed. The more you walk into this discomfort zone, the more you'll realize how it is essential to real connection. And like most things, the more you do it, the easier it becomes. When you're scared to take that first leap, just remember others will be inspired by your courage.

*In the middle
of every difficulty
lies opportunity.*

ANONYMOUS

CHAPTER THREE

Reframe

Find the Hidden Advantages

MY FRIEND JEN is an amazing gift giver. I aspire to reach her level, but I'm a work in progress. Jen always knows just what you need even when you have no idea yourself. When I was healing in the first weeks post-accident, she brought me two things: dry shampoo and Malcolm Gladwell's *David and Goliath*. The dry shampoo was a novel product then, and I didn't own any. Talk about a game-changer. This was the era when I was in a wheelchair and covered in wounds. Taking a bath or a shower was a major production—so major, in fact, that I once had my awesome mother-in-law wash my hair on the couch over a trash-bag-protected setup. So, yes, the dry shampoo was a lifesaver. And so was that book.

The subtitle of the book is *Underdogs, Misfits, and the Art of Battling Giants.* In general, the book is a series of stories about people in difficult circumstances and how they discovered unforeseen advantages within their hardships. By shifting their perspective and challenging their assumptions, often in fascinating ways, Gladwell's subjects discovered surprising strengths and hidden advantages on roads less traveled.

The opening chapter, per the title, reveals a fresh perspective on the biblical tale of David and Goliath. In his reconstruction, Gladwell describes that Goliath, though an intimidating monster of a man, suffered from gigantism. He was very large, but he had limited mobility and vision. David, Gladwell argues, though physically inferior, had a set of skills perfectly suited to defeat Goliath. In addition to being protected by the Lord (the part we know), he was an expert at aiming and firing a slingshot, which could target the highly immobile Goliath from afar. And we know how the story ended. David triumphed.

Reading Gladwell's take on how, by challenging our assumptions, we may find hidden advantages in ourselves or in our situations inspired me to think differently about my predicament. At first, my decision to be open to this kind of thinking was a desperate attempt at a coping mechanism. The months after I lost my leg were a dark, depressed time, and I latched on to anything that could help me crawl out of my hole. I vividly remember banging my fists on my bed, wailing, "Why did this happen to me?" Come winter, there were days when my depression was so deep, I couldn't take a bite of food unless I forced myself to (which was never an issue before this saga).

Hardship, and how we respond, is in many ways the very *stuff* of life. How many 90-year-olds claim that nothing crummy ever happened in their life? Hardship will find all of us at some point, and for most, it will find us more than once. It's part of the human condition. But like everything else, hardship is subjective. If you can challenge your assumptions—shift your perspective—you'll quickly learn there is more to life than what's been lost.

In fact, with your mind open to possibility, you can even find some hidden advantages in hard situations. You just have to look.

~~~

IT IS A BIT OF a wild notion that simply thinking differently, repeatedly, can have such a dramatic impact on your life, but it's true.

When I joked in the hospital the day after my leg was amputated that I'd write a book and work one day a month, I put the kernel of a thought in my mind that grew and grew. Of course, just having the thought didn't write the book for me. But, my brain was put on notice. Writing became a vehicle for me to organize my thoughts, share my progress with friends and family, and ultimately discover the backbone of what this book is about.

While in recovery after my accident, I wrote on the Caring-Bridge platform. It was a lifeline for me to my extended network of supporters, and it often filled me with the belief that I did have the stuff to write a book. As I shared insights from my journey, I was not only sharpening my writing ambitions but also continually highlighting the silver linings of my predicament.

And guess what? That 2017 TEDx Talk I gave was also pulled from the threads I started on the CaringBridge site. And all of it was made possible because I planted an idea in my mind and continued to nourish it. Throughout that experience, I had the chance to see how the whole TEDx process works, meet some amazing fellow speakers, and have an unforgettable night with friends and family gathered to watch me speak onstage. The video is not on the most-watched list or anything like that, but I still occasionally check how the views slowly tick up on YouTube even years later. I always wonder who is watching this talk of mine and hope it's helping someone to slay their dragon.

I've lived a much bolder life than I previously thought possible by purposely harnessing my life challenges for good. I never would have thought about doing a talk before my accident. And since that talk I've become a regular keynote speaker, yet again expanding on what I've learned and how I can help others. Through this unexpected path, I've found passion, purpose, and an outlet for my love of connection.

Purpose is a powerful motivator. It guides, it inspires, it discerns, it gives life meaning. There are some things that drive purpose in many of us: kids, family, faith, work.

When something life-altering happens, it is an opportunity to reveal another layer of purpose. I've met so many people who have found purpose in their pain.

This purpose isn't always obvious or even welcome at first, but over time it can provide you with a compass to share your gifts and your journey to add more meaning and depth to your life.

My purpose has been revealed to me through sharing my stories—my purpose is to share them to help others. By sharing my pain, I create empathy and understanding. By sharing my victories, I encourage belief and faith. My purpose is rooted in the idea that we should tell our stories to one another to add to our collective wisdom, to openly share our struggles and what helped us heal, and to encourage others to share their stories. When I hear someone say that something I've shared has helped them deal with a hardship in their life, it brings me joy in the way only a purpose-driven idea can.

And I've learned that sharing my story is more than just sharing with the power of words. Taking a page out of Amy Purdy's book, I did something I never would have allowed myself to do pre-injury. Taking a courageous step forward and choosing to put aside my self-consciousness, I participated as a local "star" for the annual charity fundraiser Dancing with the KC Stars. I was asked to compete in the event as the first ever uniquely abled star. I am historically a willing but terrible dancer and would likely have said no if things were "normal." However, in my situation, there was nothing to lose, only the fun experience to gain, and the opportunity to help a brilliant charitable organization and share my story through dance. And fun and fulfilling it was! My dance partner and I did a bait-and-switch performance to maximize the "aww, that's sweet she's trying" vibe before showing off what I could really do with my innovative legs. For the first part of the performance, I wore a long black skirt and we danced slowly to Patsy's Cline's "Crazy." Then the music cut, I ripped off my overskirt to reveal a bright-orange animal-print shorter skirt, and we tripled the pace with "Your Mama Don't Dance" by Poison. It was a blast!

Speaking of cool fundraisers, this leads me to the story of my friend Billy Brimblecom. Billy is the executive director at Steps of Faith Foundation, an organization that helps provide free prosthetic limbs to the uninsured and underinsured. The annual fundraiser for Steps of Faith is called Thundergong, which is a live concert and variety show.

Billy lost his left leg in 2005 to Ewing sarcoma, a rare type of cancer that occurs in bones or in the soft tissue around the bones. Billy was just 28 years old and a successful musician with a new band and a new record. I met Billy in 2020. The amputee community is smaller than you would think, especially for people in their forties, and living in the same city we had both heard of one another. We met for breakfast and instantly hit it off. Billy is a cool cat, a fierce drummer, and a lifelong sneakerhead with a burning passion for everything he pursues—and he's got good hair too.

Billy's journey from a traveling musician to the executive director of a nonprofit came through his prosthetist (the unfortunate job title of someone who makes prosthetics), who introduced him to the founder of Steps of Faith. Billy really wanted to help others face their post-amputation struggles and was inspired by the work of the organization. He was also craving to be at home more with his family. As he says, he wanted bankers' hours, not musicians' hours. He found himself enthralled by the idea of helping others in situations like his and was ready to make a change. Add all that together along with some good timing, and he decided to take a leap of faith and jump in and lead this organization. It was make or break for the nonprofit and make or break for him. He followed his heart, and a new purpose was unveiled for him—giving people promise by restoring hope and mobility through prosthetics.

From the hidden advantage lens, Billy not only found an amazing purpose that fit his lifestyle, but he has also been able to take his musician's perspective to differentiate Steps of Faith, which is where Thundergong comes in. I've been to about a zillion formulaic charitable fundraisers where you buy a ticket to sit at a table for dinner. Dress fancy. Eat a chicken breast. Watch a video. Hear a speaker or two. Yada, yada, yada. There's nothing wrong with it. In fact, I am involved with many organizations that take this approach, and it works. But Billy's creation of Thundergong is a unique live show that features celebrity guests, including the event host and Billy's friend since they were teenagers, Jason Sudeikis (SNL, *Ted Lasso*). The event features lots of music, led by a band including Billy front and center on drums and his talented wife on vocals, other amazingly abled amputees, dancing, and fun. The event is a hot ticket, and it keeps Steps of Faith rolling forward and helping people get their life back. And it enables Billy to share his purpose by bringing together two of his loves: helping the amputee community and performing live onstage.

Billy has translated a tough set of circumstances into a purpose-driven life while maintaining the unique special sauce that is Billy. And by finding purpose in his pain, he's helped numerous people find their own purpose again. I've recently become a board member of Steps of Faith, allowing me to walk alongside Billy to help others.

My childhood friend Tiffany has also found purpose in her pain. In 2015, she was diagnosed with ALS after almost two years of struggling with many symptoms and no answers. ALS, also known as Lou Gehrig's disease, is a progressive neurodegenerative disease that affects nerve cells in the brain and spinal cord. The average survival time for those with ALS is only two to five years.

Tiffany has always been a warrior. I remember her flying around the track with unparalleled speed in high school. To see her once extremely able body degenerate bit by bit is unfathomable, but Tiffany perseveres. One of the things she said in a message she typed to me, via her special eyewriter on her computer as she can no longer speak, was this: "I knew that God had his reasons, and he wouldn't give me anything I couldn't handle. He has a plan for me. I knew that I had something rare, and it needed awareness. Even if that was the only reason, I would take it on."

And she has! Tiffany has contributed to the medical side of innovation, participating in countless clinical trials. Along with her large support group, known as Tiffany's Crusaders, she's also shared knowledge about her rare condition, including by wearing special shirts and sharing details about the disease on the 19th day of every month (she was diagnosed on November 19, 2015). Tiffany continues to defy the odds and selflessly finds purpose in the notion of helping others down the road by sharing everything she's learned about a condition many doctors couldn't even diagnose for several months.

Another offshoot of finding purpose in pain is how it can reveal hidden gifts in others who are pushed to the fore when the unexpected happens. My husband has spent most of his career in sales:

selling paint for 20 years followed by selling educational software. He should have gone into the medical field. Whenever I had a wound dressing to change or even a staple left in post-surgery, he seemed to revel in the role of novice medical professional. Who knew? My daughter, Morgan, also shone in the face of adversity. Her hidden gifts? Courage and empathy. When she was only three years old, she advocated for me in the most hilarious way. I always have to wear some sort of shoe to walk. I just don't function well barefoot with my prosthetic or my other injured leg. This includes when I go into pools, so I wear water shoes to maximize function. On our first vacation post-accident, Morgan and I hopped into the hotel hot tub and some other older kid immediately called me out. "Hey, you can't wear shoes in the hot tub!" I was still new at this amputee business and was frozen for a second. Before I could respond, my little sidekick popped up and said, "This is my mom and she was run over by a boat and has to wear shoes in the water!" Case closed by the three-year-old with the courage to stand up to someone she thought was being a bully. Morgan was 10 years old when my lung journey started. At first I tried hard to not show my struggles to the kids because I didn't want them to worry. I firmly believe kids should not have to worry about their parents. Then one day, out of the blue, she gave me a hand-lettered picture that simply said, "It's okay to not be okay." Her emotional intelligence and empathy blew me away that day and in many days to follow.

Through my struggles, I've also had the opportunity to see my son's caring spirit shine. One night when I was still in my wheelchair, Mitchell asked me if he could get a stuffed animal and lie with me in my bed for a while. Normally, I would have been task-mastering on this weeknight—brush your teeth, get to sleep, and so on—but I literally couldn't do anything, so I just let the moment happen. Instead of bringing down one trusty friend, I watched him proceed to carry down about 20 different stuffed animals and carefully lay them all next to me. The real kicker was the caterpillar. I'd had this caterpillar since I was not much older than he was (he was four at the time). Believe it or not, that caterpillar lost a leg that same fall! You can't make this stuff up. He carried down the caterpillar and his detached leg and put them on the bed next to all the other stuffed animals. Watching how he didn't want to leave any of them behind and how we covered each of them up with blankets gave me the gift of seeing into his little—but very big—heart.

I realize that I am likely a little biased when it comes to assessing the various virtues of my family members. But no matter the case, having a front-row seat to watch these amazing people grow together with me and through my experiences has given me such a flush of pride and an amazing sense of just how much purpose can be found in pain.

Your pain will either be your prison or your platform. With a hidden advantage mindset, you can migrate toward the latter.

⌁

I AM REALLY GOOD at painting my own toenails. It is far easier to paint them when you can set your foot on the table in front of you! I'm also pretty good at shaving my legs—well, what's left of them.

The point I'm making is that while I certainly wouldn't have asked to have my leg amputated or my lungs replaced, there are still "upsides." Sure, I struggle to do some things now, but so what? My life before these trials is not the same life I live now. Things have changed. So, instead, I try to look (with humor when I can) at the advantages of my life as it is *now*.

When tragedy comes, you find out who your friends are. I was lucky I already knew. The people I was closest to showed up in so many functionally and emotionally supportive ways. It's a beautiful thing to know your friends will really be there for you when you need them—that's a hidden advantage. I saw this again a decade later when I had the lung transplant. During the three months I had to spend living away from home in St. Louis to be near the transplant team, I needed people to drive me back and forth from Kansas City on the weekends and to "be my keeper" during the week. I was required to have a caregiver with me during those initial months, and it was too much of a strain on my husband and our kids to have that always be him. Aaron, of course, was the caregiver in the first intense weeks, but I wanted him to have some relief and be able to keep our kids' lives as normal as possible. We had a calendar for each week, and I had others sign up for a week to hang with me in St. Louis. Between friends and family, I had 12 different people spend a week with me in less-than-exciting circumstances. Talk about feeling blessed.

I'm also fortunate to have a lifetime handicap parking pass due to my amputation. I try hard to not use it anymore, especially if someone else is in greater need, but that parking pass has saved my bacon many times. More recently, when I could barely walk due to my lung issues, it allowed me to get into doctor's appointments or other events without having to almost collapse walking into a building. Instead of seeing this pass as a bad thing, I embrace having it when I need it. On a lighter note, guess who had rock star parking during the entire World Series in 2015 when my beloved Kansas City Royals won it all? That's right, me! There was an entire row of handicap spots that hardly anyone was using, so I cruised up and took one for our tailgate.

Another small but meaningful example in my life is around showering. I have to take off my prosthetic leg to shower because it isn't waterproof and because I need to clean the part of my leg that goes into the prosthetic socket. Some amputees can balance on their "good leg," but my "good leg" also has challenges, and I don't feel stable trying to stand on it in the shower. So I use a shower chair, which sometimes can make me feel like I'm ancient. I have a couple of ways I get into the shower chair. First, I can walk in and sit down and proceed to take off my clothes and leg from the chair and gently toss them on the floor outside the shower. Then, when I'm done, I scoot closer to the door and reach out and put the leg back on with a dry towel underneath me. Classy. Another method is to crawl into the shower in the morning when I haven't put my leg on yet and then crawl back to my bedroom post-shower. Even classier. I'm not going to lie, the showering saga has been one of the biggest annoyances of my amputee life. However, I have over time discovered some real benefits from sitting down and showering. It's actually quite relaxing once I'm in the chair; leaning back and allowing the water to cascade over me is very refreshing. On the rare occasion when I'm using my waterproof swimming leg and I do take a stand-up shower, I kind of miss my chair.

No matter what, the trick I've learned is to at least let some of your mindshare think of the positives versus obsessing over the negatives outside of your control.

I've found lots of hidden advantages over the years post-accident, some big and some small. My lung journey is newer, so I'm still in the process of seeking the good that can come from this rare set of challenges. It's all still pretty raw, so I understand if this line of thinking finds you in a similar spot. The memories of feeling like I was hyperventilating simply from rolling over in bed and the zillions of scary medical tests I endured are still fresh in my mind. And on top of that is the unknown range of future outcomes that weigh on me every day. I know sometimes it can feel like there is nothing good to find, but I know from experience that's not the case, so I will continue to seek.

One major thing I have discovered throughout this experience is the meaning of the proverbial "every day is a gift" mindset. Knowing there were many days pre-transplant when my heart could have simply given out, and now, continuing to live with mortality more front and center than most, I try and pause every day to marvel at the gifts that come from normalcy. When I get to do something mundane, like drive my kids to the orthodontist or practice, I offer up silent prayers of gratitude that I am able to do something so very basic. The stuff we can easily take for granted is still a gift to me, as I wouldn't have been able to do these basic tasks just months ago.

This line of thinking also manifests in trying to ensure I live life to the fullest. Go big or go home. The Tim McGraw song "Live Like You Were Dying" hits differently now. I had heard this song a thousand times before, but I'd never had a situation where I had to really consider a condition without a finish line. One day in the shower (of course, on my trusty chair), I heard these lyrics from that song:

> "I was in my early forties
> With a lot of life before me
> When a moment came that stopped me on a dime
> I spent most of the next days
> Looking at the X-rays
> And talkin' 'bout the options
> And talkin' 'bout sweet time"
> I asked him
> "When it sank in
> That this might really be the real end
> How's it hit you
> When you get that kind of news?"

The chorus then goes on to express how this type of life disruption created the ultimate bucket-list mindset. It speaks of skydiving and Rocky Mountain climbing. Riding a bull named Fumanchu (can't you picture it?). Of being a better person by loving deeper, speaking sweeter, and finally granting forgiveness to someone. Summarized in the final line of the chorus: "Someday I hope you get the chance to live like you were dying."

Though I'm far from perfect at it, I try to be conscious of living every day to the fullest. I've found advantage is buried in the notion of celebrating the smallest things as well as thinking about the next big thing to do to celebrate being alive.

~~~

SIMILAR TO THE IDEA of borrowing perspective, I've found you can also hone your hidden advantage–seeking skills by paying attention and looking for examples beyond your own situation.

My oldest niece, Hannah, taught me a lesson on this a long time ago. She suddenly lost her hearing at age six due to a medical condition. She recovered her ability to hear through a hearing aid in one ear and a cochlear implant in the other. Her mom, my sister Angela, was the biggest advocate and trailblazer, getting her exactly what she needed. Over time, Hannah mastered these devices, so much so you wouldn't even know she suffers from hearing loss. I've watched her take out her hearing devices many times over the years when she didn't want to hear. For instance, if her younger siblings were being loud in the car while she was trying to read, she'd simply pop off the cochlear implant. Getting good sleep in a loud college dorm was no problem for her as she had the option to escape annoying noises. Hannah has embraced her challenges and modeled this idea of finding upsides in her situation.

Or take Greensburg, Kansas, population 900. It sits a few hours away from where I grew up. Greensburg is a farming community in the southwestern part of the state, and in 2007 it was devasted by an EF5 tornado (the most violent rating) that nearly wiped it off the map.

The leaders of the town decided that with so much of the town destroyed, they were going to use the opportunity to rebuild using economical and environmentally green building approaches. Or as then Kansas governor Kathleen Sebelius noted in a press conference following the tornado, "We were going to put the green in Greensburg."

As Annie Gowen reported in the *Washington Post* in October 2020, "Greensburg draws 100 percent of its electricity from a wind farm, making it one of a handful of cities in the United States to be powered solely by renewable energy. It now has an energy-efficient school, a medical center, city hall, library and commons, museum and other buildings that save more than $200,000 a year in fuel and electricity costs, according to one federal estimate. The city saves thousands of gallons of water with low-flow toilets and drought-resistant landscaping and, in the evening, its streets glow from LED lighting."

As I've learned, Greensburg didn't get everything right (do any of us?). They had setbacks and projects that didn't work out as planned. However, by and large, this community was able to take a heartbreaking event and find a path to reconstructing their town in a new way. And today, their tiny town consults with others looking to rebuild after environmental catastrophes or that are simply looking to learn what it takes to go green. They didn't want the tornado and the devastation that came with it. But look at the good they made from it.

Another example of hidden advantages is how dyslexia can create breakthrough thinking. Like any challenge, dyslexia is not a condition people would invite into their lives, but with the benefit of a rearview mirror, there is a lot of evidence of how dyslexia has positively shaped many people and the world.

Whether it's the example of Albert Einstein being able to truly "think different" as depicted in the famous Apple ads, to many other well-known successful people—like Walt Disney, Pablo Picasso, and Whoopi Goldberg—the need to get creative to succeed with their "disadvantage" enabled them to shine.

As entrepreneur and philanthropist Richard Branson said, "It is not a disadvantage; it is merely a different way of thinking . . . out in the real world, my dyslexia became my massive advantage: it helped me to think creatively and laterally, and see solutions where others saw problems."

Making lemonade from lemons is an overused phrase, but there's certainly something to it.

WRAP-UP

I have found this idea of assuming there are hidden advantages to be incredibly helpful and cathartic. It lets your brain focus on something you can control— looking for the good in a situation. It allows you to regularly seek the positive when the unexpected tends to get us stuck in the negative. It can feel like playing a game, racking your brain for ideas and examples of that little metaphorical Easter egg of goodness amid the chaos, but over time you may unearth a hidden gem that truly makes you grateful.

Most of the important things
in the world have been
accomplished by people who
have kept on trying when there
seemed to be no hope at all.

DALE CARNEGIE

CHAPTER FOUR

Dig Deep

Pursue Relentless Resourcefulness

BEFORE ANY OF my unicorn health challenges, I would have considered myself resourceful. I was scrappy. A make-do-er. A figure-it-out-er. Need to paint a craft and don't have a paintbrush? Q-tips to the rescue. Weeklong trip and just a carry-on? One pair of shoes it is. (If you've never done it, it's harder than you think.) Big party and not enough beds for guests? I'll crash on the floor. In the final hour of a road trip with a sleeping two-month-old and don't want to stop for fear of waking him up? Pee in a diaper; it'll be fine! (It was.)

Despite feeling like the queen of scrappiness, I had no idea how resourceful I could really be until craziness rocked my life. One of my first vivid memories after I lost my leg involved what my family eventually called "the crab crawl." In our house, our bedroom and all the main stuff—kitchen, living room, and so on—are on the main floor. My kids' bedrooms are on the second floor. Since they were four and two at the time, I was used to tucking them into bed every night. As a working mom, this is something I especially cherished (okay, most days); it was a special slice of the day to unwind and be together in a peaceful setting. Books, songs, prayers, back scratching, "two more minutes." I would definitely let them milk it.

When I returned home from the hospital, I was still in a wheelchair so couldn't get upstairs to do our much-needed nightly routine. I tried other methods, such as letting them sleep downstairs or snuggling downstairs with me and then sending them up. They were little, and it wasn't really working well. My husband or mom or sister or mother-in-law—whoever was around to help—would put them to bed upstairs in the "usual" way. It was devastating to have such a meaningful thing taken away from me when it felt like I'd already lost so much. It also made me—probably a little overdramatically—worry if I was missing bonding time with my kids. I would hear them asking and sometimes crying for me, and it was like ten thousand little stabs to my heart.

After a few weeks of this, I decided it was enough. I could either be sad every night at bedtime or I could figure out a way to get up those stairs with the resources I had.

In hindsight it sounds simple, but it wasn't on my radar or anyone else's at the time. My arm wounds had healed enough at this point that I was able to propel my own wheelchair. So, I drove it over to the bottom of the stairs, locked the wheels in place, and gently dumped myself out in a heap on the landing. The first time I did this I made sure my husband wasn't in the room to watch the mayhem. The last thing he wanted was another trip to the hospital. (For what it's worth, the dismount was fairly smooth.) Then I experimented with how to get up those stairs. I found I could go backward, bearing most of my weight on my arms. The technique looked like a crab crawling up stairs, hence the name. We had a little song we would sing as the kids quickly started to crab crawl with me: "Crabbbb crawwlingggg . . . we're crawling crabs . . . crab crawlin'!"

It was worth it. On days when I felt sad and hopeless (of which there were many), the night would end on a positive note because I got to feel like myself again, putting my kids to bed and having those much-needed precious moments. My two-year-old daughter was still in a crib at the time, so I would hoist myself up into a rocking chair in her room and snuggle with her and sing her to sleep. When she nodded off, I'd text my husband and he would run up and put her in her crib for the night as I crabbed down the hallway to my son's room. We would read books, say our prayers, and make up stories. Then I would get to lie with him and hear his little sleep murmurs and feel his little breath. This was literally some of the only joy I had in those days, and it was only possible because I didn't give up.

This obstacle of getting up the stairs had a very simple solution in the end. I had spent many nights being sad and angry that I couldn't get to half of my house and couldn't participate in those bedtime routines, but in that brooding was also the obsession to figure it out. Being resourceful is not a one-size-fits-all proposition. If my first attempt failed—if perhaps my arm wasn't strong enough to lift me up the stairs—I would have found another way. (Interestingly, a decade later I couldn't get up those stairs again. This time it was due to my breathing issues and eventually because I was tethered to an oxygen machine. My kids were in middle school then and didn't need to be tucked in anymore, so I didn't need to find a solution for getting up the stairs that time. Instead, we were resourceful in a different way, developing new nighttime routines amid these new circumstances.) Bottom line: being resourceful means being open to all possibilities.

An example of this came when I was first diagnosed with my lung condition. I had no idea what the next year would bring.

Every month, week, and sometimes every day the situation would change. It wasn't easy, but I tried to keep my mind open to possible solutions to this unexpected, life-altering plot twist.

At first we had high hopes there would be a therapeutic solution that could open up the blood vessels in my lungs to reduce the pressure that strained my breathing and the right side of my heart. For a few weeks around Christmas, we tried a few different pills, but they weren't strong enough to dilate the blood vessels as we'd hoped. In January, after almost a month of feeling like I could barely move without my heart rate spiking and panting horribly, I signed up for the next level of intervention: the lifelong pump. This was not a happy choice to have to make. But I wanted to live a high-functioning life. Being short of breath from walking a couple paces was not the life I longed for. However, by agreeing to use the pump, I knew I would be enduring a radical adaptation to life as I knew it.

As mentioned, the pump is about the size of a brick and half as thick. It was hooked to a plastic tube permanently attached to my chest via a Hickman line, which is a chest port for accessing major veins. The line was literally threaded through my jugular. I am the kind of person who doesn't even like to carry a purse; often I'll just put my ID and a credit card in my pocket. Even as a grown adult. Now here I was with the pump and all its componentry.

A friend of mine (the same great gift giver who gave me *David and Goliath*) brought me ten or more stylish fanny packs and backpacks to haul this thing around. I tried to keep an open mind and embrace the idea that I could use these accessories to make the situation a little easier. They gave me stylish options for "going out," which I wasn't doing much of as it was a major hassle. I was trying to convince myself this thing wasn't that big a deal.

But the pump came with other constraints too. The pump itself wasn't water resistant, and the line in my chest, which had a sterile dressing, had to be covered completely. I've already described how big an ordeal washing myself is, and now I needed to pivot again. Of my showering options, the one where I scoot to and from the bathroom without my prosthetic now had to be done while also carrying my little pump friend with me. I felt like a toddler awkwardly crawling around while clutching her favorite toy. I learned that, once in the shower, I could place the nonwaterproof contraption gently outside the shower and run the tubing through a tiny little slit in the shower door. However, the waterproof patches they give you to cover the port in your chest do not work well, which means you have to change the sterile dressing after the shower if it gets wet, which is a major pain. So, then I tried applying some Glad Press'n Seal to the area and putting a hand towel over my shoulder. Constant grinding. Constantly working to find a better solution.

During this same time, I also widened the net to see if there were other ways I could help my own healing. A neighbor and friend of mine is into natural and holistic healing, and I had an open mind to listen to her advice. While continuing to do what my traditional doctors told me, I concurrently explored my neighbor's advice. I went to a wellness clinic that provides nutrition recommendations based on your condition. This person told me to eat only meat (really, protein). One hundred percent carnivore. I tried. Not for me. I felt nauseous. Another person told me to eat only vegetables. Another expert said to eat only high-alkaline foods. Needless to say, this exploration seemed to be a dead end with everyone giving me different and often conflicting advice. In the end, I just followed logical healthy eating guidelines and made my own decisions.

But I kept at it. I saw a holistic doctor, who did a series of tests on me around potential food allergies and hormone levels and such. This didn't yield much either. I had zero food sensitivities except a slight issue with bananas (which ended up being ironic as that was the only "food" I could have beyond my feeding tube formula in the form of a prebiotic made of banana flakes). I tried lots of supplements that were well intended but left me feeling overwhelmed and, again, nauseous as my body was already undergoing so much. One was supposedly made from antelope fur or something. But I persisted. My neighbor friend had experienced a dramatic turnaround in her health with these holistic modalities, and I have many other friends who have also experienced success in this arena, so I kept my mind open. Plus, I always think about the broader world and history and how different types of treatments are common in other parts of the world and were used for centuries before our time. Who's to say what's "normal"?

The last stop along this alternative medicine path was a woman who focused on energy and energetic solutions. I found her to be extremely helpful, as much with the mental aspects as the physical. She gave me hope and new ideas. I am grateful to my friend for helping me find her.

I traveled these paths alongside the traditional Western medicine paths, which I followed to the hundredth percentile.

And this was only the first few months of the lung journey! Somehow, I was doing all that while mom-ing and wife-ing and working.

Persistence. An open mind. Grit. Creativity. The hard but necessary ingredients of being relentlessly resourceful.

The first week of March, I had a follow-up with my awesome pulmonologist. I thought we would just discuss continuing to turn up the pump-distributed medicine to higher doses. That had been the plan—keep gradually increasing until you find the dosage that allows you to breathe easily without your body having a negative reaction. I likened it to those little analogies you get when you're pregnant: "Your baby is now the size of a grape."

"Your baby is as big as a lemon." I would say about the pump medicine, "I started at an ant. I am currently at a small frog. Some people stop at rabbit, some at deer, and some at elephant." That was more fun and easier for friends and family to digest than rattling off rates of nanograms per minute.

The medicine had helped me some, but not a great deal. In that appointment, my very caring doctor told me he had hoped for dramatically better results and that I might be the minority case who doesn't effectively respond to the medicine. In that appointment the "T-word" (transplant) was seriously addressed for the first time. I've heard people describe the moment they heard the words "You have cancer," and I have to think my feelings were similar. The world stopped. My eyes filled with tears. I was in a daze. Just weeks before we had discussed how highly unlikely a transplant would be. And here I was, now facing the likely need for a transplant.

After some numb moments and a little time to lick our wounds, Aaron and I had to get open-minded again. What were my options? We visited all the best hospitals. Talked to all the national experts on my condition. Drove hundreds of miles. My sister, who was incredibly supportive, flew with me to the East Coast. Most of these travels involved one of them pushing me around in a wheelchair as my ability to walk was fading fast. The answers were similar at each visit and aligned with those of my main care team: "You'll probably need a transplant."

The hospital I normally go to in Kansas City is fabulous. I can't say enough good things about the facility and the team there. However, since they currently don't offer lung transplants there or anywhere else in Kansas City, we had to explore where we would go to potentially get a transplant.

During our very first appointment with a transplant team at a different and renowned hospital, the first thing we heard is that a person has a 50 / 50 shot at being alive five years after a lung transplant. I had avoided Google, so I didn't know these stats. To say that's a scary thing to hear is an understatement. What are you going to do though? As my trusted friend and medical professional told me, you're looking at the wrong odds. The likelihood of being alive in five years if you *don't* do something is significantly less.

So, an open mind was required again. How do we do this? How can I not only be in the 50 percent who makes that first major milestone but be an outlier overall? Where do we go to do this surgery? What can I do to put myself in the best possible situation? I believe that being hopeful and optimistic is critical to physically healing. When you hear time and again how bad your situation is, you must be an independent thinker to see there is light at the end of the tunnel. If you don't have an open mind, it's not possible to see these outcomes. (It helps, too, to be a faith-driven person.) You must keep your mind open to all possibilities and keep pushing to find solutions in unexpected corners. Sometimes this kind of thinking can defy logic or conventional wisdom, and other times it boils down to a simple solution that was only revealed by grinding to get to the best answer.

So how do you become more resourceful? There is a lot of research on this topic, but from where I sit, the best thing to do is to actively work at it. Be conscious of when you are giving up or mentally closing doors. Ask yourself if there are paths worth exploring that you haven't considered. You don't know what you don't know, so get advice from all corners and don't dismiss things too quickly just because they don't align with your usual thinking. The core molecule that makes up the medicine that has helped so many in my predicament was thought to have less than a 10 percent chance of success when Martine Rothblatt purchased it from a major pharmaceutical company. But, after weighing her options, a 10 percent chance of success was 10 percent more than she had at the time, so she went for it. And thank goodness she did! I try to remind myself that for every unicorn circumstance there is a unicorn solution.

~~~

AN UNOFFICIAL MANTRA of the US Marines, made even more famous by Clint Eastwood in the movie *Heartbreak Ridge*, is a concept I have found very useful: improvise, adapt, and overcome. This is a shorthand definition for resourcefulness.

For me, I parse this phrase to mean "face reality head-on and know that you must adjust, keep an open mind, be willing to course correct, and believe you will succeed." Like anything, the more you do it, the easier it gets.

It might not have been a challenge on the magnitude of military action, but with hindsight I can see that even if I wasn't thinking this at the time, the saga of buying a pair of shoes for the first time post-amputation fits neatly within the improvise, adapt, and overcome framework.

When I was still in a wheelchair but starting physical therapy, my therapist told me I should get a new pair of tennis shoes. He directed me to a special store and recommended a certain brand. My friend from my hometown who also now lives in Kansas City took me on this adventure. I used to buy new tennis shoes every few years. I wasn't a runner or major fitness enthusiast, so I wore flip-flops and work shoes and just about everything *but* tennis shoes most days. I tried to get excited about channeling a new sneakerhead life, looking online at all the fun fashion items. I'm a women's size 11, so I'm used to a little shopping restriction. But nothing prepared me for this shopping trip.

We get to the specialty store as recommended and I pick out lots of cute options only to find none of them would fit on my foot.

This wasn't due to my new prosthetic—that foot was designed as a medium size 11 just like my regular foot. It was because at the time I had to wear a bulky brace on my right leg. The brace had a thick plastic piece that went under my foot and all the way up the back of my calf and was held in place with Velcro straps on top of my foot and around my knee. This brace helped me walk straighter as I had yet to undergo my tendon transfer surgery. All of this plastic added so much bulk to my foot that I couldn't get anything to work. When we had just about given up, the salesperson told me there was one model that might work. Picture the 92-year-old mall walker shoe. If you're 92-ish and still cruising steps around the mall, awesome. But at 36, I wasn't ready to slip into the weekday mall-walking circuit. However, it was the only shoe that could be jammed onto my foot. (Know that you must adjust and keep an open mind . . .) One hundred and thirty dollars later, we left with a functional but ugly pair of shoes.

I'm no fashionista by any stretch of the imagination. However, wearing these triple-extra-wide, hospital-white sneaks every single day for months was putting me over the edge. The real kicker was my friend's New Year's Eve wedding that same year. This whole leg brace and accompanying sneakers became a wardrobe obsession for me leading up to this epic wedding. (I say epic because the bride, my friend Ashley, is the funniest and most social person you can imagine, so the event was going to be a blast.)

I remember during the wedding shower being jealous of the women gabbing about the kinds of footwear they were considering, while I sat there thinking, *Should I wear the bright white clodhoppers or the bright white clodhoppers?*

I'm not a vain person, but my inability to feel like myself began to compound the depression I was already feeling in general. I started to contemplate not even going to the wedding.

It all just seemed like too much work to talk to people and figure out what to wear and the logistics of navigating stairs . . . the whole ball of wax. But I had to go. I had been good friends with Ashley for over 15 years (now 25!) and she was an amazing friend to all. Shame on me for even considering skipping.

So, I decided to do the very best I could to feel normal considering the less-than-normal circumstances. I went online and discovered Zappos. (I do not get paid to endorse them, but the store helped me so much in those early years. I not only used the standard filters, I actually called the company and found out there were all of these extra behind-the-scenes filters that are now consumer-facing but weren't in 2013.) After an entire afternoon of shoe selecting, I ordered 20 pairs and hoped for the best. Twenty pairs of shoes that were within the clodhopper range but masked as black dress flats. I'll never forget the look on my husband's face when that massive delivery showed up.

Aaron (hesitant and confused): "Did you order *all* of these?"

Me (not breaking eye contact): "Yes."

A few evenings later I sat by our Christmas tree and opened 19 boxes. I couldn't get a single pair on my braced foot. I did have a contingency plan, as is often required in a resourceful mission. The twentieth pair had the exact same specifications as my white sneakers. I had checked every dimension. These guys were the black mall-walker Hush Puppies version. I put them on, and, as expected, they fit. So at least I had a black shoe. I then sadly returned the other 19 to their boxes to be shipped back. *Wah-wah.*

Time was ticking as the wedding was nearing and I didn't have an outfit to go with these new shoes. I didn't want to wear a knee-length dress; I was a hot mess of white and black plastic and metal on my lower half and I wasn't used to all of this yet. The idea of wearing a longer dress stressed me out because I was terrified of tripping. That left pants, which were tricky to put on and fit with all my parts and my swollen and healing limbs. So again, I turned to online shopping and ordered every pair of black wide-legged pants I could find. I had to have them within days, so shipping speed was a top filter. When all those pants arrived, only one pair slipped over my legs. I wasn't price sensitive at all in this state of desperation, and of course the one pair that fit were $500. And they were ugly!

The night of the wedding, I got my hair done and put on makeup and tried to pretty myself out of my depressed state. I strapped on those mega pants and my men's Hush Puppies. In a last-minute dose of inspiration, I even got a black marker and covered up the mall-walker white reflective circle on the back of the shoes to ensure they were as unobtrusive as possible. My husband and I went to the wedding and reception, and it was as lovely and fun as I thought it would be. Though it may seem silly in the scheme of things (what to wear to a wedding), I really had to dig deep to at least feel somewhat comfortable that night. On our way home from the reception, I realized how much I had needed a fun night out to break me out of the Groundhog Day I was living. I was so glad I didn't give in to the bitterness and miss celebrating a friend and celebrating life.

Oh, and later that week, I returned those $500 pants. At the wedding I tucked in the giant tag. I had never done this before, but I felt like the universe owed me one. When I do speaking engagements I tell people that if I come clean about this at least a few hundred times, I can let myself off the hook!

Keep an open mind, know that you must adjust, believe that you will succeed.

One more example of this comes from, of all things, snorkeling.

During the "easy" years between year one of my amputee life and nearly a decade later getting the lung diagnosis, we took a family vacation to the Cayman Islands. I fell in love with the crystal-clear water and white sand beaches. When you go to the Caymans, there are a few things you have to do if you want to really suck the marrow out of the experience. Go see the sting-rays at stingray island. Check. Open an offshore bank account. Check. (Just kidding!) Snorkel in some of the most beautiful water on earth. Check!

Before the leg challenges, I had snorkeled a few times and absolutely loved it. As we approached our trip to the Caymans, I at first assumed I just wouldn't participate, but I really wanted my kids to take in the experience. The reason I assumed I wouldn't snorkel is because I can't wear flippers—a core part of the snor-keling ensemble. Neither of my ankles flex as one is metal and the other is partially immobilized through surgery. The act of flipping in flippers requires ankle flexion I do not have. (There are prosthetics that do allow for ankle flexion of this type, but I didn't need this and hadn't explored it since my other foot wouldn't flex anyway.)

With my problem-solving brain humming, I started to chal-lenge the assumption that I would be unable to go snorkeling. My ankles don't flex, but I could improvise. What if I simply skipped the flippers and used my arms to move me around instead? What if I wore a life jacket to further buoy myself in the water as I just wanted to float near the surface anyway? So, I packed my trusty water shoes, a life jacket, and my old snorkel gear and decided to give it a try. Yes, despite not living near an ocean, we do own snorkel gear because Aaron is grossed out by the shared gear the typical booze cruises use (and rightfully so!).

When we got to our hotel, I went down to the beach and gave my custom snorkel approach a try in the shallow water. It worked brilliantly! I simply swam with my arms instead of my feet and the rest was the same. By the end of the trip, my kids even ditched their flippers because they thought my way was superior.

Because I was able to improvise and adapt, I enjoyed seeing some of the most beautiful fish and reefs I had ever seen. And, I enjoyed an unforgettable afternoon with my family.

Being resourceful isn't rocket science. As Albert Einstein said, "It's not that I'm so smart, it's just that I stay with problems longer."

~~~

ONE OF MY all-time favorite quotes is from Arthur Ashe: "Start where you are. Use what you have. Do what you can."

I like that the quote pushes you to simply begin, which as we all know can be the hardest step. When I do my speaking engagements, I always challenge people with this quote. I ask each person to think of the thing they are waiting to begin. Maybe it's to pursue a college degree. Maybe it's to repair or walk away from a strained relationship. Or to start exercising. Or to move to the location of their dreams. Or to find a way to help with an important cause that seems too big for one person to make an impact. Or maybe it is simply to clean out their closet.

Whatever it is, most people can conjure up something in their mind they are putting off that they know they should be starting. The challenge is simple—give yourself a deadline to take one active step forward. It might be next Monday, next month, or the first of the year. Whatever you choose, stick to it, and begin where you are with what you have. The momentum will carry you forward, and when you're stuck, begin again.

I've found this idea of not waiting for the perfect circumstances is key to being resourceful. It's so easy to use less-than-ideal circumstances to put off progress. For instance:

When I lose some weight, I'll go hiking in Colorado.

When we hire a few more people on the team, we can start that new desperately needed work.

When the kids are out of the house, we'll take that trip.

Or, as I could have thought after my accident, *When I am fully healed and walking, I'll go upstairs again.*

Rarely are circumstances going to be perfect, so you just have to get after it from where you are. Waiting to have the resources—whatever they may be—isn't always possible.

Not having one leg and having an injured second leg equates to a lack of key resources. Those circumstances weren't going to change, so it forced me to get resourceful early in the leg journey. Same thing with my lungs. I had no option; it was all instantly permanent. Each time I began where I was, because where else can you begin? I have found, as I'm guessing you have too, that anticipating a thing really is harder than doing it. I'll also admit I'm not always great at this myself. It's so easy to put things off that seem hard to start. I can rationalize procrastination with the best of them. Give yourself a little grace, but set that deadline and stick to it.

It's the third part of the quote, "Do what you can," that really is a saving grace. By doing what you can, you enable yourself to start without stacking the chips against yourself right from the outset. If you want to begin running, your goal might be to do a marathon one day, but you don't start there; you do what you can. By making it okay to do what is possible by your own estimation, you can see progress faster, which enables you to accomplish your goals sooner. The flywheel will start turning, and each subsequent movement will feel easier than the first.

There is a lot of turmoil in the world right now; I guess there always has been. The issues of the day are just different. Most of us feel passionate about one or many of the issues facing society.

I think for many of us, it's hard to imagine how you could make even an ounce of difference, so it's easier to just do nothing. *What can I really do to help millions of hungry children? Where would I even begin in the fight to end sex trafficking?*

Do what you can. Beautiful simplicity. If we take a little slice of the problem and attack it proactively, that contribution, when combined with others, adds up to a meaningful difference. As philanthropist Percy Ross neatly stated, "Many drops make a bucket, many buckets make a pond, many ponds make a lake, and many lakes make an ocean."

During the months leading up to my lung transplant and during the transplant process itself, I spent more than 50 nights alone in the hospital. As any parent would, I hated being away for that amount of time and craved ways to stay connected with my kids. We would text and FaceTime and just old-school talk on the phone. The basics were fine, but I could tell it got kind of monotonous for them. It wasn't like I had a lot of news to share—at least, news that was appropriate to share.

One day when I called Morgan's phone, she answered in this hilarious monotone voice and introduced herself as "Dontavious," Morgan's personal assistant. I asked to speak to Morgan and she rattled the phone and then came on the line as herself. She is a wonderfully unique bird, so this is the kind of thing she does. I had no idea how this little joke would create really fun bonding moments for us in the weeks to follow.

To increase the fun factor, I started to text Dontavious to schedule time with Morgan. Her replies would crack me up: "Morgan is available tomorrow at 1:30 but otherwise she has a full day of appointments." From there we developed an entire world, all from my hospital bed and wherever she was at the time. We decided Dontavious was a squirrel, so we found an online image that we felt represented his personality.

Since Morgan was now quite famous in our fictional world, we also created "Sebastian," her personal security guard. The tough-talking, poor-spelling Sebastian was of course an octopus with multiple limbs to protect her. All while sporting a pair of dark sunglasses. An adorable hedgehog was her social media manager. She did yoga with the 103-year-old iguana "Francis Turtlesmith," who was quite fit for her age.

This whole crazy train we hopped on made texting and phone calls so much more fun for her and for me (because I knew she wasn't just calling Mom out of a feeling of obligation). We started where we were (sadly apart from one another), used what we had (phones), and did what we could (made up our own imaginary world to add fun to our days).

It's fun to see how this whole thing has further inspired her natural creativity and performance skills. She is in theater for the first time this year in middle school and loves it. She just wrapped up her debut role as the Cheshire Cat in a production of *Alice in Wonderland*. She also continues to develop some of our original characters, along with others. Ashley (aka the New Year's Eve bride) is also game for this kind of silliness. She joined in our story and created "Chip," Dontavious's wild cousin. We occasionally get videos sent from Chip. Hilarious. At least to us!

If the specifics here sound too weird to you (as Aaron and Mitchell would vote!), digest the generalities. What can you do to spice up your current situation and make it better, even if it just buys you some temporary help?

I busted out this bag of tricks again recently when Morgan had a fever and wasn't feeling well. With my immunocompromised state, I have to be careful around sick people. So, when she was feeling a bit better, we decided to go outside to the front porch and chat while sitting a good distance apart. We played an improv game where I provided prompts and she created skits. We were on that porch for two hours with the crazy characters she created! It made us both feel better about our current states.

With Mitchell, we stuck to more of the traditional kinds of communication. It was amazing, though, to read what he wrote in a few cards to me. He's always had a huge heart (he used to open gum wrappers and write me notes and then reseal the gum!), but in this middle school–aged era, he isn't always as forthright with his feelings. The little notes he wrote in those cards to me were words I read and reread and reread again. I thank Aaron for taking him card shopping to get him new tools to "use what he had."

When the usual topics of school and sports got played out, I decided to take a little bit of interest in his video games. Under normal circumstances I tolerate video games, but I'm not interested in hearing the details or watching him play. However, when I couldn't be there physically, I found I would do just about anything to connect. I started asking about the games he was playing at the time, and he would tell me details about *Madden* (a football video game) or *The Show* (a baseball video game) or whatever, and I could see and hear him light up that I actually cared about this dimension of his world. It also helped me understand that these games are incredibly sophisticated. He knows so much about players and plays and stats and odds and all kinds of things. I had no idea. It also reminded me that sometimes you have to enter into someone else's domain to foster deeper connection with them. When I was able to come home, I spent an entire afternoon in his room (in a chair he sprinted to get me) and watched him play game after game. I just loved being near him and not in another hospital bed.

Start where you are. Use what you have. Do what you can. Thank you, Arthur Ashe.

～

WE OFTEN THINK we must figure things out alone. No one wants to feel like a burden, so it's hard to ask others for help. The irony, however, is many people want to help. You just have to get out of your own head and be okay with simply asking.

My cardiologist friend, Jon, saved my life. If I hadn't called him in desperation when I couldn't find answers to my heart and lung problems, who knows where I would be right now. I read that my condition is so rare it often takes months or even a year to get a proper diagnosis. I didn't have that kind of time, so I am eternally grateful that my friend is an amazing doctor who partnered with another amazing doctor to figure out my condition in a matter of hours.

Aaron and the kids would have struggled so much more if I hadn't been comfortable asking friends and family to take shifts staying with me in St. Louis.

My leadership team and peers at work were incredibly helpful in both of my journeys, from urging me to take a break when I was very sick and trying to still work, to helping me make connections at hospitals, to helping me transition back to work in the best way for me. They prayed for me and cheered for me and took the burden of work off my shoulders when I needed to focus on my health.

My sister drove to our house the second I called her the night of *the call* ("We have lungs for you"), arriving after midnight. She took care of everything, even taking Morgan to her competitive volleyball tryouts all weekend while I was in surgery. My parents spent many days and logged many miles helping us. My mother-in-law did our never-ending laundry and dishes, bunking in our guest room for weeks on end as she lives over four hours away.

So many friends and neighbors gave our kids rides to and fro when we were dealing with my stuff. This made it possible for Morgan and Mitchell to continue to be involved in their activities even when we couldn't get them there.

It's hard to be vulnerable enough to ask, but other people have resources they want to share. I've discovered we all have different resources at any given time. Some have money, some have time, some love to cook, some have flexible schedules, some love to pray, some know medical information, some are just great mentors, and on and on. Widen the net of the resources available to you by asking others to share their resources with you. Then when it's your turn, share your resources right back. It's a gift to receive, but for many it's also a gift to give.

WRAP-UP

Resourcefulness is key to unlocking solutions to challenging problems. It will take some grit and grinding and some trial and error, but finding solutions to hard problems is possible and so very rewarding.

*Don't spend a lot of time
imagining the worst-case scenario.
It rarely goes down as you imagine
it will, and if by some fluke it does,
you will have lived it twice.*

MICHAEL J. FOX

CHAPTER FIVE

Check Yourself

Don't Assume Your Assumptions Are Valid

I'LL NEVER BE *able to hold my daughter while standing up again.*

I'll never be able to go on vacations that require a good deal of walking.

I'll never be fully happy again.

I'll have to deal with this clunky leg brace for the rest of my life.

My physical limitations will stop me from taking care of my kids as I've hoped, and they will not be as close to me as a result.

I will never wear normal shoes again.

I'll have to change my job to one that doesn't require any travel because I'll have too many challenges.

These were just a few of the assumptions I made after losing my leg that proved to be false. Now I have a mental list of worries about my new life post-lung transplant, and I'm confident many of them will be proven wrong. That doesn't mean I don't freak out some days due to the gravity of the situation, especially when there are few distractions and I'm lying in bed at night or when the slightest thing feels off. It's hard not to think of worst-case scenarios when worry gets triggered in your brain. Having fears and worries is a natural and expected part of grief and grieving—especially in the face of extreme adversity. It is difficult *not* to think about what is lost or could be lost because of severe hardship. However, this is where challenging assumptions and shifting your perspective is essential—otherwise, you may never get out of the grief spiral.

What I've learned through my ordeals is that negativity is easy and humans are generally pretty terrible at predicting the future—myself included. There's an old saying attributed to many luminaries that I think sums this up best: "I am an old man and have known a great many troubles, but most of them never happened."

My friend Luis has found himself in this worry cycle—for good reason—but gained wisdom about how to live life in the midst of challenge.

Luis is one of those people who just exudes charisma. He has a warm smile and mad soccer skills. His Colombian upbringing shines through in his gregarious, generous nature and positive attitude.

During the time I was struggling with my lung diagnosis, Luis was facing a monster of his own. He had noticed an uncomfortable lump in his lower abdomen and eventually found out it was a tumor from a rare type of cancer called synovial sarcoma. Upon further scans, nodules were also seen in his lungs, leading to the assumption from various top doctors that his cancer had spread. At 36 years old, with an amazing wife and four children under the age of 10, Luis was told he had a year or two to live.

How does one cope with the information that they won't get to see their young and vibrant family grow with them? That they won't make it to their fortieth birthday?

Luis's answer: live day by day. Focus on one day at a time. I had given him this advice as I was desperately trying to use it myself. Luis, however, embraced it and lived it better than anyone I've ever met. He put my approach to shame! He explained his thinking to me:

> Day by day. One day at a time. That's one of the most powerful things anyone has said to me. It's something you've heard before, but it doesn't make sense until something like this happens. My brain was thinking things like, *Let me start writing emails to my daughter because I may not be here when she's 15.* I made myself get out of that line of thinking and practiced thinking only day by day and sometimes moment by moment. Book the appointment. Take the kids to school. Celebrate the win I got today. One thing at a time. It wasn't until I made this shift that I really started living life.

I'm thrilled to report that Luis's medical journey ended in a miracle beyond belief. It was discovered that the nodules in his lungs that were almost certainly related to the cancer were indeed not. He had a successful surgery to remove the original abdominal cancer and was deemed cancer-free. His doctors said he is the only case of this type of cancer they have ever seen that has had this result.

Even though Luis is not living the daily struggle anymore, the day-by-day notion has changed him forever.

> I used to think I had to think about my life goals in chunks of 5 years, 10 years, 15 years. That's what everyone tells you to do.

I don't do that anymore. I just take what is happening and build from the ground up. I live in the moment until I'm living in the next moment. I have scans coming up to make sure the cancer isn't reoccurring. I'm not letting myself worry about that. It's on Thursday and today is Monday. Tomorrow night I have a championship game with my soccer team. Thursday will come and I'll do the scans then.

Thinking too much about the future can rob today's happiness. I wish I could put this day-by-day notion in a bottle and give it to my kids. This wisdom is huge but hard to come by.

Aaron and I have borrowed a similar mental framework from the Navy SEALs: "Stay in your three-foot world." This basically means "focus on what you can affect right now." During times of stress, pressure, or worry, focus on what you can control in the moment and ignore everything else.

People would ask me all the time, especially when the medical situations were the most acute, "How is Aaron?" And because of this way of thinking (and his natural ability to compartmentalize situations), I was able to confidently say—most of the time—that he was okay. And I meant it. I don't think people believed this or understood how that could be the case, but Aaron is a master at staying in that three-foot world, and that is his way of handling the tough situations.

This approach allows him to avoid the inevitable assumption-making about the future. Sure, he's tempted to do so, like all of us, but he has the mental model to redirect those thoughts when they come.

Mitchell is also someone I look to for inspiration when I find myself silently slipping into catastrophic worrying. He is a naturally calm and even-keeled kid, one of those people who never gets too high or too low regardless of the circumstance. I admire this trait, especially how he has it honed at such a young age. It's part of his old-soul wisdom. I've observed how he uses rational thinking and statistically probable outcomes in his decision making. Where my brain can naturally slip into, *They didn't answer the phone. They must be in a ditch somewhere!*, his brain considers a more likely explanation. As an independent thinker, he has an innate ability to question the built-in assumptions of any given situation, cut through the clutter, and quickly and succinctly come to his own conclusions. Like his father's ability to stay in his three-foot space, Mitchell's logic-based thinking offered me another model to emulate in the hardest of days.

Whether you take things day by day like Luis, focus on what you can control right now like Aaron, or logically check your worries at the door like Mitchell, consider ways to stop the negative assumption cycle in your brain. At different times, I have used all these strategies (sometimes in the same day!), along with a lot of faith and optimism, to see me through the negative and back to positive thinking. You can too.

Another method I've discovered is the power of gratitude to lessen the inevitable worry cycles. I've often tried to keep a grateful disposition, but post-transplant I've taken this practice to the next level as I try and live out the "every day is a gift" mindset I mentioned earlier. Several times a day, I take a purposeful pause to express gratitude. For instance, I will take a moment when I'm walking somewhere to stop and pause and just be mindfully grateful for a few seconds. To acknowledge my health. To thank God for the miracles in my life. To recall harder days that create an elevated appreciation for the normal days. To just look up and breathe. To recognize something so basic, such as: *this is awesome, I can carry my own lawn chair to the baseball field again.* I recently heard this insight: it is impossible for your brain to feel grateful and fearful at the same time. This is true in my lived experience and it makes me even more committed to developing an attitude of gratitude.

<center>~~~</center>

MY SURGEON SCARED the crap out of us moments before my double lung transplant. And it was 100 percent my fault.

In the weeks leading up to getting on the transplant list and having the surgery, I talked to a friend of a friend who had a double lung transplant at the same hospital four years prior. She told me her surgeon said to her, "Don't worry. You just go to sleep and we've got the rest. These are *great* lungs."

So, when my highly accomplished and experienced surgeon came into the pre-op room, literally seconds before I was transported to the operating room, I asked him, "The lungs are great, right?"

His response: "They're good enough."

Record scratch. *What?* Aaron and I were dumbfounded. Needless to say, it wasn't the best way for us to part before one of the scariest moments of our lives.

As they wheeled me back to the operating room, I rationalized that in a medical context it would make sense to communicate in a pass/fail, black-or-white type of way versus offering a value judgment. And that is exactly what my surgeon meant—the lungs were viable, which is what he needed to determine before the surgery.

If, as I previously stated, we aren't very good at predicting our own future actions, why do we think we can accurately predict the actions of others?

A lot of research around interpersonal communication points to the idea that assumptions are at the heart of many miscommunications. Whether we're conscious of it or not, our assumptions of others are typically based off our own past experiences and our own likely actions and preferences, not the other person's.

We see the evidence of assumption-based miscommunications everywhere, including in the tools that are meant to help us solve this problem. For example, preference-based personality tests are sometimes used in the workplace to help avoid miscommunication via assumptions. You may prefer a casual mode of interaction whereas someone else may do better with scheduled time to discuss a topic. Without knowing it, you can drive someone nutty by interrupting them just because you assume they don't mind a quick chat.

In the popular book *The Five Love Languages*, Gary Chapman warns against projecting our own assumptions on others. The concept aims to close the assumption gap, helping people in relationships understand how the other person feels most loved, as this isn't something people always communicate effectively. For instance, if you are an "acts of service" person, you may feel more loved when your significant other unloads the dishwasher versus gives you flowers.

Text messages are also notoriously fertile ground for assumptions and miscommunication. Without the help of nonverbal cues, tone, or context, we may leap to conclusions that are completely incorrect. And those conclusions tend to be the negative ones as opposed to the positive. Our assumption meter tends to round down.

So, back to my surgeon. I retrospectively put myself in his shoes: He was getting ready to do a 10-hour, life-or-death surgery. He was going to be leading an entire operating room full of other surgeons, nurses, anesthesiologists, and other medical staff. His demeanor that morning could have easily been the equivalent of a pregame routine, similar to an elite athlete preparing for an event. And there I was, assuming his mind would be focused on my emotional health, ready to feed me platitudes like "It will all be okay," because that's what I would have done. Plus, I didn't know his personality at all. I'd never even met him before that moment. Perhaps the tone I received was just who he is. And to be fair, he didn't yet know the outcome of the surgery, and medical professionals aren't usually the type to pontificate without concrete information. But I charged ahead, assuming I could get him to say, "Don't worry, these lungs are *great*."

I now know these gifted lungs of mine *are* great, but I created unnecessary mental havoc by trying to re-create someone else's moment. I falsely assumed I could control the situation and get served the words I longed to hear on a silver platter. Who knows what organic great thing could have happened pre-surgery if I hadn't done that?

It's important to be conscious of when you're making assumptions. If they go unquestioned, you can hold on to them as fact when, in reality, they are simply things you think are true.

Take this story as an example. After a lung transplant, it's common to have anxiety about breathing without supplemental oxygen again. You become so used to having this crutch that you stop trusting in your ability to breathe "room air," as it's called. This makes sense because when your lungs are failing and you lack oxygen for even a moment, it is the worst feeling in the world. It's like you're instantly drowning. This happened to me a couple of very memorable times.

One time I was at Mitchell's basketball game and went to my car to get a new oxygen tank. I was still learning how to hook up the contraption because Aaron had done it for me before. (I'm not very mechanically inclined.) He had shown me how to do it, so I thought I was okay, but I had a little issue getting it all hooked up correctly as I switched tanks. As I was trying to put the gauge on a fresh tank to release the oxygen, it started leaking and not flowing through the tube to my nose. While this was happening, it started raining on me. This whole saga lasted less than a minute, but my body started to freak out. Thankfully, I was able to fix it despite my mounting anxiety. I sat in the car for a bit after, huffing and puffing and coming down from that scare.

After a transplant, you suddenly have lungs that are capable of breathing normally again (miracle!), but based on your past traumatic experiences, you just don't trust them. When I moved out of the intensive care unit, I was still receiving supplemental oxygen, at the lowest possible flow. It was just my *woobie*, my reassurance. I didn't physically need it, but I thought I did.

The first night in my new hospital room on the step-down floor, my nurse pulled a tricky and wise little move. He was a wonderful nurse, a 24-year-old young man with great medical knowledge and a caring heart. He was so earnest, I would have never guessed he would pull a move like this!

While I was sleeping, he turned off my oxygen but kept the cannula in my nose. The flow was so low I didn't even know it was off. The next morning as I sat there with my placebo oxygen, he asked me if I wanted to take it off. I assumed I needed it. I told him I didn't think I was quite ready. Then he revealed to me it had been shut off for the past several hours.

Really?! He hoped I wasn't upset. I told him I thought he was brilliant.

He nudged me to believe in myself and the ability of these new lungs. My assumption that I needed the supplemental oxygen was holding me back. Thank goodness I had my nurse to challenge me!

～～

JIM CARREY, at the time a young wannabe actor and recent factory worker with a ninth-grade education, did an incredible thing.

Sitting on a hilltop on Mulholland Drive, he wrote himself a $10 million check for "acting services rendered" and dated it for Thanksgiving 1995. He carried that check around in his wallet as a constant reminder of his dream. Sure enough, five years after he wrote the check, but before his deadline of Thanksgiving 1995, he was paid $10 million to star in *Dumb and Dumber*.

In an interview with Oprah where he talked about the check and the power of visualization, he also gave a nod to the hard work he put in during the five years between writing the check and cashing it. As he said, "You can't just visualize it and go eat a sandwich."

A clear and audacious goal, using positive assumptions as fuel. And a work ethic to make it happen.

When we are faced with something hard, most of our assumptions are on the negative side of the ledger. It's human nature to worry about what may come, especially in the middle of something difficult and unknown. When I find myself spiraling into negativity, I imagine my desired future state.

In the early days after my amputation, I would envision myself walking again, without effort or pain.

When I learned I could no longer eat food, because my new lungs were susceptible to being infected by bacteria aspirated into them from my esophagus, I would envision myself eventually eating a meal again with my family around the table.

I routinely imagine myself speaking on a big stage, not just with my disrupted legs showing but also wearing a T-shirt with neon-pink-outlined lungs.

I turned the words from a friend into a mantra during my transplant journey: "I just know, this is not how your story ends."

Like Jim Carrey, by assuming that I would succeed, I was able to imagine the future I wanted. That, in turn, helped me to navigate the hard days.

The strategies I employed—visualization and positive self-talk—are two surefire methods of shifting your perspective that have been scientifically proven to work. The subconscious is an incredible thing. Visualization has been proven to increase strength and athletic and musical performance and to induce feelings of positivity and gratitude. Positive self-talk, mantras, and trying to maintain an optimistic outlook are proven to reduce anxiety, increase self-confidence, and even to speed recovery time in rehabilitation.

I have my own little Jim Carrey story, though it is admittedly not as grandiose. However, it is important to me and hopefully an example to you that your future visioning doesn't have to land you a movie deal to be considered successful.

I've talked about the seed that was planted to do my TEDx Talk and speaking work. But I also said in that hospital bed a decade ago that I would write a book.

Though it took me eight years to begin, I manifested this idea early on, and not just in the one-liner in the hospital bed. A mere six weeks after the accident, I contacted an author I had recently met at a work event and asked if she would mentor me. She said she couldn't take on any more work at the time because she was finishing up another book, and she couldn't believe I was thinking about this so quickly after a life-altering incident. In hindsight, it was way too soon to be thinking about writing, but it was the same brand of audacious thinking that Jim Carrey exhibited. During this same era, I set up a new email account and used a password that involved the idea of writing a book. Every time I had to enter that password, it watered the seed. Over the years, I would jot down thoughts and ideas, capturing what I'd learned and where I'd stumbled. I paid attention to other people's books and made mental notes of other people's journeys.

Baby steps. Water droplets. And eventually, here is the book! Whether you are the seventeenth reader (following my family and friends, who must read it) or the seven thousandth reader doesn't really matter. What matters is I had a goal that I slowly and surely manifested by putting in the work, and eventually I made it happen.

As famous author and radio personality Earl Nightingale said, "Plant your goal in your mind . . . Care for it. Work steadily towards your goal and it will become a reality."

~∿~

A POPULAR THEME that emerges when I'm asked questions at a live event is how to care for others. "What do I do? What do I say? What helped you?" I always love these questions because they remind me how many caring people are out there.

My advice is always simple: As the one being cared for, don't be afraid to say what you need and what you don't need. Don't assume your circle will think you are a burden. Going back to Kelly's insight about not wanting to be a burden by revealing her struggles in caring for her son Ryan, I can relate. I tend to be a people pleaser, so it's hard for me to make requests or set guidelines for people trying to help. With that said, I've found it's super helpful to people to simply be up front about things. Most people truly want to be helpful, and any guidance you can give them helps both of you.

I learned this lesson most explicitly from my friend and coworker Nicole. She was out of work for a while battling cancer (which she crushed!). When she returned, she sent out an incredibly helpful email simply stating what is and isn't helpful for her. I found it refreshing and useful, and I wish I had known sooner how to do the same. For instance, two phrases that really bothered me in the early days of my accident devastation were "I'm so sorry" and "new normal." I was trying to stay positive, but hearing people say "I'm so sorry" made it hard to think of anything but the dumpster fire that had become my life. *If everyone sees this as such a train wreck*, I thought, *then it must really be a complete train wreck!*

I was working my way to the point where I could see myself as a battle-scarred warrior, not a helpless victim. The term "new normal" sounded like this to me: "You will eventually get used to these terrible circumstances, just wait." Ugh. (Some folks, I know, find comfort in both phrases—and there is no judgment here. Different strokes . . .) Also, I should have known better than to assume these caring people thought my circumstances were a dumpster fire. They just didn't know what to say!

If I had known enough to write a note like Nicole did, I'd have probably written one to my circle saying that we don't need the meal train. The meal train, if you're not aware, is a way for friends and family to sign up to provide meals to the person in need without doubling up on the kinds of meals or having too much food one week and not enough the next. I love the sentiment and thoughtfulness behind it. For our family, however, we wanted to feel as normal as possible, and eating other people's food all the time did not feel normal (the occasional food drop-off is nice, but we didn't need it every night). Plus, we felt wasteful if we didn't eat everything we received, whether we liked it or not. As an outsider, though, why would you ever assume we *didn't* want the meal train?

Clarity is kindness. Telling your inner circle of friends and family that you don't want their help in the way they are offering it takes vulnerability and courage, but when it's said with grace and gratitude, it will be a gift to those who truly want to help. Unexpected situations require help from others, so don't feel bad about asking for what you do need. And again, the more open and honest you are, the more targeted your support can be, and the more helpful others can feel.

Moving to the other side of the coin: for those who want to help someone else, show up in some way and be specific with your offers to help. A commonly used, but not super helpful, phrase is "Let me know if there is anything you need." First of all, that puts the work of contemplating ideas or asking for help back on the person you're trying to help. And don't assume they'll know what you can provide. Narrow down the options to what you are able and willing to offer so they can choose what will be most useful.

When trying to be helpful, I think we've all wondered things like, *Will I be invading?* Or, *What in the world do I say?* What I always tell people is simple: "Just show up." Really, that's the big headline—be vulnerable enough to walk alongside the awkwardness of hard situations. That can mean dropping off cookies at the porch or front desk, sending a card, sending a care package, offering to just sit and listen, gifting a restaurant gift card, texting an inspirational quote, picking up kids from practice, mowing the lawn, feeding the pets, renting a hotel room near the hospital for the main caregiver, and so on.

Don't just offer to do something, *do something*. And don't worry about whether the something is perfect. It won't be. It's not on you to have the perfect idea or the perfect words. More often than not, those are not achievable goals. Once you do something, try to read the tea leaves on if what you did was helpful or not and adjust from there. And to the points above, if the person hasn't said what they prefer, just ask. I've found as both recipient and helper, it's useful to ask specific versus open-ended questions. Words like "We all help each other" also help soften the feeling of being a burden that people tend to have during these seasons.

Here is an example to tie it all in: "I really want to help because people were so helpful to me when X happened. Would you prefer some homemade meals? Or can I organize a house cleaning service?" Or, "It makes no sense for all of us to wait in the pick-up line. Could I pick up your kid tonight from practice? It'll make me feel better when I need help when Y travels for work."

I will also say this, as it's a good reminder to counterbalance the negative news we hear every day: when you are in a time of needing help, it will strengthen or restore your belief in humanity. There are so many good people out there with big hearts.

"What is the use of living, if it be not to strive for noble causes and to make this muddled world a better place." WINSTON CHURCHILL

AFTER MY SCRAPPY college days and early into my professional working life, wanting more than a luck-fueled trip to the Alamo Bowl, my friend Tressa and I decided we were going to travel to Europe. Neither of us had been before, nor did we have families who had traveled internationally, so we were naïve to the whole scene. We used a travel agent, who hooked us up with the right flights, hotels, and trains for our 10-day adventure to London, Amsterdam, and Munich. This was not going to be a hostel-filled backpacking excursion, the kind many of our friends had done in college. We were young professional women, and we were going to travel like it.

But a funny thing about assumptions is how powerful they are if you don't check them. So, picture this, two career women staying at nice European hotels and lugging everything they brought for 10 days in giant hiking backpacks! I have no idea why it didn't dawn on us that the roller suitcases we used when traveling anywhere else would make sense in Europe too, but nope, we borrowed giant backpacks and crammed everything into them because we *assumed* that was how one traveled to Europe. Still makes me laugh to this day.

So does this: My first job in a corporate environment was as an intern for an insurance company. Growing up in a farming community, I didn't have much experience with this type of workplace, so everything was new to me. I loved my boss and knew she had her twenty-fifth anniversary coming up because everyone was talking about it. The math seemed right, so I assumed this was her twenty-fifth *wedding* anniversary. I had never heard the word "anniversary" used in relation to job tenure. So, on her big party day at the office, I gave her a card with a picture of a little boy looking lovingly at a little girl on a swing, inscribed, "Happy Anniversary!" It was so awkward! (And for added embarrassment, a coworker discovered my mistake and teased me about it for the rest of the summer!)

Again, why? Why did I make this silly choice? It was a failure to check my assumption. The problem is that when we are assuming, we aren't always aware that we are assuming. We take in some data point and extrapolate a conclusion, which leads us to take a certain action. The data point I had here—my boss is celebrating her twenty-fifth anniversary—was correct, but how I interpreted that point was obviously incorrect, leading me to a mistaken conclusion and embarrassing resulting action.

Being aware of how we form assumptions is important to help us check the validity of our assumptions. The best we can do is to take a step back in the moment and consider alternatives to the assumption being made. Do we have all the data? Are there potential blind spots in our interpretations? Are there other viable conclusions? This is a tricky exercise, because as bad as we are at predicting the future, we're just as terrible at confusing assumptions with facts.

While those two examples above were funny little mistakes, here's an example that was much more serious. And one of the craziest experiences of my life.

It's not entirely uncommon for your heart to have some arrythmia after a major surgery like a double lung transplant. It's even more common for someone like me, whose hypertension, which created so much pressure on my heart, was suddenly relieved by having new lungs that worked well.

My heart event happened a few days after my transplant. I had the surgery on a Thursday. To help manage the dramatic shift in heart pressure, my surgery was performed using an ECMO (extracorporeal membrane oxygenation machine). Because of this, I was in a medically induced coma longer than most other transplant patients. The medical team tried to wake me up on Saturday, but I was in too much pain and was incredibly agitated. Aaron's memories of this experience are traumatically vivid, but mine consist of only a few fuzzy fragments, including listening to audio from my son's baseball game. (I love baseball, so my husband played his live game in an effort to distract and calm me. The pain was too great though.) The decision was made to reintubate me, and I was "asleep" until Monday, when my wakeup process went more smoothly. I did have to be intubated—while awake—for several hours, which was harrowing. I kept scrawling my desires on pieces of paper, with less-than-stellar handwriting in my anesthesia fog.

Once the tube was out and I was more relaxed, I was desperate for good sleep. My body was beyond exhausted, but I couldn't fall asleep, which is typical in a hospital. I asked for some drugs to help me sleep better. Melatonin, the first-line go-to, wasn't working on me come 2 AM. So, they offered the next step up, which I later learned is actually an antipsychotic (but is also a regularly prescribed sleeping med). I was not used to the medicine, so it hit me hard. Thanks to the high levels of anesthesia medicine and steroids in my system, I was already seeing weird things when I closed my eyes, like psychedelic tiger patterns and tessellations, and now I was seeing blurry versions of them. I felt completely wasted, but sleep was starting to come. Just as I was fading off, my nurse looked at the giant TV broadcasting my vitals and her eyes became huge. She sprinted out of the room, and there was a lot of commotion. Next thing I knew, they were injecting a syringe of medicine into my IV to stop my extreme arrythmia.

Do you remember the famous scene in *Pulp Fiction* where Vincent plunges a giant needle into Mia to stop her drug overdose? That's the best way to describe what happened next. The second that medicine hit my bloodstream, my body lunged forward, and I lost all bodily control for that half a second. It was beyond wild— and was even wilder in my psychedelic tiger mode. But it worked, and my heart rhythm returned to nearly normal.

Nearly normal. A day later I had moved out of the ICU to a stepdown room when my second arrythmia happened. Given the change of scenery, the nurses and some of the doctors were different. They were still monitoring my heart carefully, and things looked fine until about 2 AM (this must be my heart's time to howl). The arrythmia wasn't as dramatic this time, but it was still something that required intervention. The drug that was used in the ICU happened to start with the letter A. The drug they recommended to help me the second time also started with a letter A, and it had a similar-sounding name in general. When I heard the name of the recommended medicine, I assumed it was the same thing I'd been given the night before. Since I figured it would give me another *Pulp Fiction* moment, I immediately refused. I was freaking out. The medical staff was so gracious, helping me think through my options and advising me while reminding me I was the ultimate decision maker. After 10 minutes of thoughtful discussion and literal hand-holding with the doctor, I decided to trust their recommendation and steeled myself for another Mrs. Mia Wallace moment.

Tears were streaking down my face when my wonderful nurse Paul said, "Okay, here we go." Nothing. I felt nothing! And then he mentioned it would take about 10 minutes to administer. The other drug took about a tenth of a second. I was confused. We then consulted my chart and discovered they were not, in fact, the same drug. Though the situations were similar, the first round of arrythmia was much more extreme, requiring a more extreme solution. I had no idea there would be two different drugs that could treat arrythmia, both with similar sounding names and starting with the letter A. I lacked data and context and assumed I knew. All this drama, discussion, and dread could have been avoided had I realized I was making an assumption but presenting it as a fact. (And for what it's worth, the medical team now better understood why I'd gotten so distraught, and that felt good.)

I liken it to this relatable situation. What tends to happen when you Google medical symptoms? In my experience, every site basically leads you to "You will die in 48 hours. You surely have flesh-eating bacteria" or something equally dire. So, you learn to avoid Googling symptoms. Stay off the internet for medical diagnoses! There isn't enough context, so you end up in algorithmic assumption land. But before you learn this lesson, you have to worry about that flesh-eating bacteria.

False assumptions can have harmful repercussions. The problem is, when you're struggling and the reality you see is overtly negative, not challenging your assumptions can hurt you. You owe it to yourself to check yourself. Don't assume; it makes an ass . . . you know the rest.

WRAP-UP

Making negative assumptions about our future is human nature when the chips are down, but it's not helpful. You really don't know what will happen until it happens. Do everything you can to consciously shut off the part of your brain that wants to dwell in that unknown negative space. Or as my sister wisely says, "Don't go borrowing tomorrow's trouble."

If you can't fly then run,
if you can't run then walk,
if you can't walk then crawl,
but by all means, keep moving.

MARTIN LUTHER KING JR.

CHAPTER SIX

Be a Riser

Realize Your Resilient Nature

THE CHAPTER-OPENING QUOTE is on the wall at the entrance of a high school gymnasium just down the road from me. I happened to be at the gym on a day when I really needed some inspiration—I'll get to that later—and like all King's writing, this quote is packed with meaning and inspiration for and beyond its original context. He had a way of crafting words that touch each of us. At Hallmark we call that "universal specific writing." Simply said, we all share in the human condition, and there are truths that are specific to us yet experienced by many. This notion comforts me that we are all together in this thing called life—even if we experience different seasons at different times.

(Before I go on, if you haven't already, I highly recommend you read King's "Letter from Birmingham Jail." Doing so will allow you to experience the wonder of his beautifully crafted and intensely powerful words. Thanks to my friend and author Tara Jaye Frank for that tip.)

To literally parse King's quote, it has a very specific meaning for me. Once I had my leg accident, running was off the table—ironically, not because of my prosthetic; I'm sure you've seen those amazing running blades. It's my right leg, my "good leg," that cannot run. The missing tendons and bone, and partially immobilized ankle, just don't work that way. Thankfully, I wasn't much of a runner anyway, so at least I had that going for me. I do hope to never be chased by some wild animal though. I would definitely be the first one of the herd taken down!

For a while, of course, I couldn't walk either. The months I was in a wheelchair were incredibly humbling. Navigating the world is difficult in a wheelchair, and as a short-term wheelchair user, I lacked the right setup and know-how, making me a pretty unsuccessful user. As a result, I was often reliant on others, and I've already discussed how hard it is for me to feel as though I'm a burden.

Suffice it to say, walking is a huge gift that people—myself included—routinely take for granted. I was made painfully and acutely aware of this when dealing with my pulmonary hypertension. Due to my extreme shortness of breath and resulting pressure on my heart, walking was difficult. I'll never forget when I needed King's words most. In that gym with his quote on the wall, I was trying to see how long I could walk without stopping while another mom practiced volleyball with her daughter and mine. I was due for another six-minute test at the hospital, which is exactly what it sounds like: you walk as far as you can for six minutes, and they measure your distance and relevant vital signs. I had yet to complete the six minutes without stopping, and I desperately wanted to work my way up to doing so. This was the era of having the medicine pump and hoping for more improvement. I paced the gym back and forth that day, having to stop to breathe by the three-minute mark. It was humbling. I was embarrassed and sad. After that day, walking got even harder as my condition deteriorated. I got to the point right before I went on oxygen that I could only take a few steps before I had to stop and catch my breath. At a volleyball tournament just weeks later, I could barely make it to the restroom. I kept having to stop to rest and catch my breath. To cover, I tried to master the look of someone purposefully pausing all the time, pretending to watch each game along the way at various courts as if I knew or cared who was playing. Every step was a struggle.

And then there is crawling. I crawl. Every day. Still. Ten years after losing my leg. I probably always will. Since I don't sleep in my prosthetic leg (for many reasons, including comfort, needing it to charge, etc.), I am legless in the night. As I've said, I can't rely on my other leg to successfully hop or use crutches, so my choices are to crawl to the restroom in the middle of the night or put my leg on and take it back off. I've done both, but I've discovered crawling is quicker and easier. Luckily, the crawl from my bed to the restroom is a pretty short scramble, but the mechanics of getting up and on and then off and down from the toilet is a sight to behold. You know that feeling when you have to pee but don't want to get out of bed and deal with it? That is exponential in my world.

When I was plugged into my pump in the pre-transplant era, the crawling got even more complicated. Not only did I have my brick-sized pump and cord along for the ride, I also had to consider the tube in my nose feeding me oxygen. My crawl is already awkward, and having to do it while lugging the pump and maneuvering the wires and tubes so I didn't get caught up or pull anything out was too much. I finally cracked and had Aaron resurrect the bedside commode I'd used in the first months after my amputation. What a devastation that was! My basement is like a medical apparatus archive, and occasionally some of yesteryear's tools need to get dusted off and put back in rotation. Reintegration is something I'm very stubborn about and resistant to. But it got to the point where I had no choice. Aaron is very accepting of all of my medical stuff, but the bedside toilet is his most hated thing in this world—for good reason! But we hauled it up. We kept moving forward. What else could we do?

It is important to point out here that it is okay to be angry, to be depressed, to lose hope. I've certainly occupied all these territories, multiple times each. Don't beat yourself up over the need to take a rest, to hit the pause button, to have a little pity party. It's okay to get down, just don't stay there.

The last part of the MLK quote, "but by all means, keep moving," reinforces that you mustn't give up, even if you've stopped and rested for a bit. Don't slide back. You must rise. Rise to the occasion, whatever it may be.

The notion of rising was captured beautifully in a song I listened to a lot on that pulmonary rehab treadmill. Sung by Dierks Bentley and written by Travis Meadows and Steve Moakler, the song is called "Riser." As you read the excerpt below from the chorus, notice how it can be used as an affirmation or an aspiration—both are powerful.

> I'm a riser
> I'm a get up off the ground, don't run and hider
> Pushing comes a-shovin'
> Hey I'm a fighter
> When darkness comes to town, I'm a lighter
> A get out aliver, of the fire, survivor
> I'm a riser

I was texting with a friend about writing this book, and she sent me the following words that neatly encapsulate the reality in the messages of both King and "Riser." I'm sharing her words here with her permission:

> Bad stuff happens, and you don't want to get out of bed. But then you think of your kids, and you rise. Life knocks you down and it all seems too hard, but you find a way to rise. Christ suffered. He died. Then he rose. We all suffer. And we rise. And in the rising we find what matters most to us and unleash focus on that which is truly important. Isn't that the gift of sadness and trauma? That it makes us realize what matters and it makes our true purpose rise to the front of our focus versus being buried in the background.

Whatever you can find in your life to make you a riser, despite the circumstances, focus on that. And when you do—when you rise, even if only for that moment—you are building resilience one block at a time. And that will make it easier to rise again and again.

Over time, by rising against hardship, pain, or distress, which, no matter how charmed the life, will impact each and every one of us, you will build resilience.

In this way I believe resilience is like immunity. When you have a child, at some point they are going to get sick. Colds, flus, runny noses that never end, all of it. And each time they get sick, these germs build their immunity. The point is you must go through sickness to build immunity.

The same is true for resilience. I'm not saying you should seek out extra hardship if it hasn't come your way yet, but you can learn a lot by being aware and conscious of how any challenge you are facing could be helping you to build some resilience muscle. And any challenge is good enough to draw from. It doesn't matter if your challenge seems to pale in comparison to another person's challenge. Challenges are relative and shouldn't be compared anyway. If you find the situation challenging, then it's a challenge. End of story. When times are tough (and only you can decide when that is—it is personal to everyone), allow yourself to *feel* the challenging aspects of your situation. Allowing yourself the vulnerability to accept that you are being challenged is a form of rising, of being resilient, of moving forward.

It's been interesting for me to reflect on how much stronger I am mentally during my lung journey than I was with my leg journey. Many things played a role in this, but one factor is surely the resilience I have built from dealing with the initial challenge of losing a leg and the resulting daily adaptations. Having gone through this experience makes me more confident that I can handle whatever may come my way (to a degree). Knowing I have faced demons before—and even death twice—and have continued to move forward helps me believe I can rise when it counts, even if I need to spend some time down first.

By the way, that dreaded bedside toilet has been moved back to the basement. I sure hope it doesn't find a way to rise again!

~~~

MY FRIEND HOLLY has suffered with infertility for years. Like Kelly, whom I highlighted in the chapter on vulnerability, she decided to vulnerably and courageously share her story with others. Her words, quoted from a social media post, were accompanied on that post with a photo of a home pregnancy test reading "not pregnant."

I quit. My heart can't break any more. This is infertility. Four years, four months trying to conceive. Three pregnancies, three miscarriages. MILLIONS of tears. Thousands and thousands of dollars. So many doctor appointments, tests, emails, documents, conversations, and sleepless nights spent researching. We're so tired. No, we're exhausted. Mentally, physically, financially . . . exhausted. BUT—then I hear the whisper—*but you're meant to be parents . . . don't walk away from your dreams . . . you can do this . . . just keep going*. It's a roller coaster you just want to get off. This is what infertility really looks like. Big hugs to all of you that just keep going. You inspire us. One day it will be our turn. I'm here to normalize every negative test result.

When I spoke with Holly about resilience, her words resonated with me and supported the notion of moving forward: "Although your heart has been shattered over and over again, you continue to get up and move forward. It's not because you want to," she said, "it's because life didn't give you a choice. You look to others that have survived, who are a little ahead of you on the journey, and you draw strength from their toughness, their resilience. People that have experienced terrible things have remarkable empathy. They can hold space for your *hard* in a way that others cannot."

Holly's words reminded me of a quote attributed to Elisabeth Kübler-Ross that I received after my accident from my best childhood friend, Mandi. It was engraved on a wooden sign that I've since hung in my home: "The most beautiful people we have known are those who have known defeat, known suffering, known struggle, known loss, and have found their way out of the depths. These persons have an appreciation, a sensitivity, and an understanding of life that fills them with compassion, gentleness, and a deep loving concern. Beautiful people do not just happen."

I love the notion that hardship can create beauty. Just like a diamond can't be created without pressure, some gifts can't be revealed without challenge. When we find a way to be resilient after struggle, even if it takes time (which it almost always does), there is a bounty of empathy that resides alongside that new well of resilience.

Holly and her husband, Jimmy, took to yard work and manual labor to help sweat out their sadness, and unsurprisingly, they created something beautiful from their pain. They demolished fences, weeded, regraded the lawn, planted new sod, and built 250 feet of fence, completely redoing their backyard. "We poured our grief into exhausting our bodies. It was the only way we could fall into bed every night completely exhausted so we didn't have to think about how bad our hearts hurt," Holly told me.

The result was that their manual labor transformed their backyard into a way to honor their hardest memories. In the perfect spot in their newly remodeled yard overlooking an unbelievable view of the Colorado mountains, they planted a tree to honor the three babies they lost to miscarriage. As Holly shared in a second post on their journey, "All winter I prayed that we gave this tree enough water and protected it from the wind and snow to survive this past year. Today I noticed how much it has grown. Although it looks dead, if you get close, you can see the growth and the new blooms. That's how I feel today. Like this past year was a dead season, but I've still grown. I'm still grateful. I'm still alive. You might need to look really close to see my blooms, but they're still there."

I'm grateful to Holly for sharing her story of struggle and resilience, and I know by her sharing, others will be able to borrow her perspective. Again, it's a virtuous circle.

〜〜

*"Think of a packet of seeds scattered in the garden.
Some seeds get more sunlight, more water, and are
planted in nourishing topsoil, and because they
are put in the right place at the right time, they can rise
from seed to seedling to a thriving tree. Seeds planted
in too much shade where they don't get enough water
may never become anything at all, unless someone
transplants them—saves them—before it's too late.
Then there are those seedlings that look for light on
their own. They creep from the shade into the sunshine
without being transplanted. They find it without
anybody digging them up and placing them in
the light. They find strength where there is none.
That is resilience."* DAVID GOGGINS

IF YOU DON'T KNOW who David Goggins is, he's worth looking
up. From a hardscrabble upbringing to becoming a Navy SEAL
to being one of the world's most elite ultra-endurance athletes,
Goggins knows a thing or two about resilience.

What I like about his quote, however, is how succinctly he
captures society with his seed/seedling metaphor.

We have all met some thriving trees—those folks who seem
like they were born with a silver spoon, or at least had most
of the advantages needed for a successful life afforded to them.
This is not to say they never endured hardship or needed to be
resilient, but the good life certainly seems to come easily to
some people.

Similarly, we all know those unfortunate seeds who were
never given a chance because of the circumstances they faced

or the predicament they found themselves in through no fault of their own. There are occasions when, plucked from their plight and transplanted, these individuals have thrived—and we know those people too.

And finally, we have also met the seedlings—those who, against all odds, "find strength where there is none." It is this latter group—the seedlings—I want to focus on, because as Goggins says, that is where we'll find resilience.

In writing and researching this book, it became obvious to me that so many people who have had a global impact have come not from the thriving trees of life but from the seedlings. (And to be clear, I'm focusing on resilience. I'm not judging anyone's character or endorsing the ideologies of any of these well-known people.)

Take J.K. Rowling, for example. She was newly divorced with a newborn baby and living on government assistance in the UK before her first Harry Potter book was published. She had a dream she wouldn't give up on, and she struggled mightily to reach it. In order to pitch her novel, she used a typewriter to manually type each manuscript she sent out because she couldn't afford a computer or the cost of photocopies. Today, the Harry Potter series has sold over 500 million copies and produced an entire movie and experiential franchise. "The knowledge that you have emerged wiser and stronger from setbacks," Rowling told the Harvard graduating class in 2008, "means that you are, ever after, secure in your ability to survive. . . . We do not need magic to change the world, we carry all the power we need inside ourselves already: we have the power to imagine better."

The power to imagine is exactly what Walt Disney became famous for. He survived a poor childhood, lived through the Spanish flu, and dropped out of school at age 16 to help in the war effort. After being denied by the army due to his age, he forged his birth year so he would appear 17 and became an ambulance driver with the Red Cross in France in 1918. Not three years later, Disney opened his first animation studio, but despite working with other visionaries of the time, the company went bankrupt. Essentially penniless, Disney moved to Hollywood, and the rest, I guess you could say, is the stuff of fairy tales. Think of the joy Disney movies, songs, and experiences have brought to so many lives. What if Walt had given up? "All the adversity I've had in my life, all my troubles and obstacles, have strengthened me. . . . You may not realize it when it happens, but a kick in the teeth may be the best thing in the world for you."

Nelson Mandela certainly endured more than a kick in the teeth. He spent 27 years as a political prisoner in apartheid-era South Africa. Instead of causing him to give up, his time in prison steeled him even more to bring peace and justice to a racially divided country. Mandela was freed and negotiated the end of apartheid, earning him a Nobel Peace Prize in 1993 and delivering on his determination to bring justice, democracy, freedom, and human rights to all. He then became the first democratically elected president in South Africa's history.

While many may know the 2009 film *Invictus* about the 1995 Rugby World Cup held in South Africa, the name of the film is derived from a poem by William Ernest Henley. "Invictus" is Latin for "unconquerable," and it is said that Mandela routinely recited the poem to his fellow inmates. It is also said that the poet, Henley, was, in part, referencing the struggles he faced and the resilience he showed after losing a leg to tuberculosis. This poem, in its entirety, is the stuff of resilience.

Out of the night that covers me,
Black as the pit from pole to pole,
I thank whatever gods may be
For my unconquerable soul.

In the fell clutch of circumstance
I have not winced nor cried aloud.
Under the bludgeonings of chance
My head is bloody, but unbowed.

Beyond this place of wrath and tears
Looms but the Horror of the shade,
And yet the menace of the years
Finds and shall find me unafraid.

It matters not how strait the gate,
How charged with punishments the scroll,
I am the master of my fate,
I am the captain of my soul.

I could go on and on about other famous people as varied as Abraham Lincoln, Malala Yousafzai, Thomas Edison, Eminem, Oprah Winfrey, or Bethany Hamilton to help make my point that the seedlings—those who have struggled valiantly against the odds—have managed to change and shape our world, but I'd like to look closer to home.

When we speak of "the Greatest Generation"—technically, those born between 1901 and 1924 (or 1927, depending on your source)—we are talking about a group of individuals who endured hardship the likes of which we will hopefully never see again. They endured the Great Depression and provided the bulk of the soldiers and workers for WWII. It was a *generation* of seedlings. I would argue there is no other time in modern history when people had to become so resilient—to become a generation of risers.

Jewish citizens in Europe who were oppressed and persecuted faced circumstances most will never understand. Yet many of them showed a spirit of resilience beyond comprehension.

The Allied soldiers who signed up to risk their lives to be a part of the solution, willingly storming beaches razed with gunfire or dropping out of perfectly good airplanes—so much resistance. So much resilience.

The people left on the home fronts to fill in the gaps also had to rise to the occasion.

I knew three of my grandparents, and they all faced challenges in their lives that made them resilient. My grandma Opal, my dad's mom, was born in 1908 and lived to be 102 years old. She passed away the same week Morgan was born. I spent a lot of time with her as a kid, eating her buttered noodles and mowing her lawn. I marvel at how much she lived through in her life. Anyone who lived during this particular slice of history experienced massive changes in society. She rode a horse to school yet lived through Y2K. Grandma also had a lot of personal experiences in her life that required resilience. She lost her mom and a newborn sister to the Spanish flu when she was just nine years old. She helped run a restaurant that catered to the local community and was the place that held the big celebrations for soldiers returning home from World War II. She spent an entire month in a chair with just a light sheet on her body to help her recover after being badly burned by an exploding pressure cooker. Despite all this and much more, she was calm and jovial. She always had a joke, delivered with her dry sense of humor. I once asked her the secret to living so long, and she said, "Walk every day and don't get worked up about too much."

My grandparents on my mom's side were just outside of the Greatest Generation, being born in the early 1930s, but they exemplified the same traits as that generation. My Grandpa Russell was one of five kids, and he was a twin. Gramps was the first twin born and had straight hair but his twin had curly, so he would always say his brother stayed behind to get his hair curled. Ironically, his twin became a barber. Gramps had "made it" by the time I was on the scene. My sister and I spent a lot of time with Granny and Gramps, and he was always super fun. He'd let us drive before we had a driver's license. He'd buy us giant cookies and soft pretzels. He was a jokester and loved to wear brightly colored pants and drive Cadillacs. People loved his fun personality. But before all this fun, he worked around the clock because he didn't have two pennies to rub together and had to find a way to provide for his family. He started a business with nothing but hard work, a dream, and good instincts. After many twists and turns, he turned that business into a great success in his life. Granny helped build that business while raising four daughters and battling multiple health challenges over the years. Granny was also very hard-working, both in the business and in the ways she would show us her love. She sewed my sister Angela and me and our cousins dozens of homemade Barbie clothes that were incredibly sophisticated and intricate. She grew up (very happily) wearing dresses made from burlap seed bags, but our Barbies had fur-lined cloaks. She made birthday cakes for everyone and (along with Gramps) never missed a school performance. She passed away just hours before I got the call for my lung transplant. I believe she played a role in my miracle because she always found a way to do anything for anyone despite her challenges.

My grandparents, and probably many of yours too, experienced massive changes and hardships but kept moving forward. I was lucky enough to witness many chapters of their resilient lives and to hear about the chapters I missed. This group of people weren't called the Greatest Generation for nothing; they are the Greatest Generation because a lot was expected of them and they rose to the challenge of the day. Like those seedlings looking for light, they found strength where there was none. Or maybe it was the other way around. Maybe because of the struggle and the required resilience, this generation had the opportunity to become great.

 WRAP-UP

In a nutshell, resilience is the ability to bounce back from difficult times in life. It is the art of never giving up. It is an earned and learned set of skills resulting from difficulties faced, both big and small. When you find a way to keep going, you get stronger and are better able to handle challenges. You don't have to be a victim of your circumstances; you can be a riser.

*If I have the belief that
I can do it, I shall surely acquire
the capacity to do it even if I
may not have it at the beginning.*

MAHATMA GANDHI

CHAPTER SEVEN

Engage Your Soul

Find a Way to Believe

FIVE MONTHS AFTER the boating accident, we went to Mexico to celebrate Aaron's fortieth birthday. I love birthdays. I love my own birthday, and I love to plan birthday celebrations for my family. I had planned this trip months before the accident. We had rented a beautiful villa on the cliffs overlooking the ocean in Puerto Vallarta, complete with a private pool and chef. I had invited Aaron's sister and brother and their spouses to celebrate with us. (Aaron doesn't like to be in the spotlight, so no big parties allowed!)

In those first days in the hospital, Aaron's immediate thought was to cancel the trip and try to get our money back. This is his way of thinking—always logical and forward-looking, risk-mitigating. My first reaction was a visceral response to keep the trip on the books. Even in the fog of a traumatic accident, I knew I would need something to look forward to in the days ahead.

I also had this belief deep down that I'd be able to go, and things would be okay. Thankfully, he conceded and we didn't cancel the trip.

As the days clicked by and the trip approached, I know that several times he questioned whether it made sense to try and go to Mexico. Considering the circumstances during that window of time, his concern made complete sense. I was barely walking again and just weeks before we left was still relying on a walker or crutches most of the time. My mental state had deteriorated. The lead-up to the trip had taken us through the dark of winter and was coupled with the depression that had set in as the grieving process ran its course. Even I started to question whether the trip was a terrible idea.

But we went. And it was the best medicine I could have imagined.

Day one: Bright sunshine. Vitamin D. Ocean breeze. Fresh margaritas and chips and guac upon arrival. Bedtime around 5 PM (early morning flight + challenged walking + margaritas)!

Day two: ATVs through the mountains! I could drive by this point, and since this kind of adventure didn't require walking, it was perfect. I do remember my thumb was struggling that day from my arm injury, as you have to hold your thumb down on the throttle continuously while driving an old four-wheeler, but I did it and it was so fun to be out and about. We also spent time that afternoon in our private pool. I didn't have a water leg yet, so Aaron would "fireman carry" me to the bathroom or wherever I needed to go. Amazing meals to follow.

Day three: Zip-lining! The reason I chose Puerto Vallarta for this trip was because Aaron loves adventure. Unlike me, he can't just sit around on a beach all day. He gets antsy and hot and bored. So, this location was a good compromise because it is near the beach and mountains and has lots of adventure options. He and I had gone by ourselves before and experienced the epic zip-lines, so I knew he would love to share this with his family.

With my challenged mobility, I assumed I would just hang out at the villa while the rest of the gang went zip-lining. I never want to hold anyone back, so I wasn't about to let the whole group miss the experience. The day before the zip-lining excursion, Aaron and I reversed our roles: now he was the one nudging me to consider participating. At first it sounded crazy. Sure, going down the zip-line is easy. But getting to the zip-line? You climb 20 or more towers to attach to each zip-line. That sounded nearly impossible to me. But Aaron believed in me, and his belief grew in me. So I went.

I'll never forget the feeling of riding that first line. Seeing that beautiful scenery and feeling the wind in my face made me feel more alive than I had felt in months. Being able to participate in something so adventurous so quickly after the accident steeled my belief that things were, in fact, going to be okay. It was like it bought me another 30 miles of runway in my belief vision, which is what I needed to keep propelling forward.

I had to push myself to believe. I had to be pushed to believe. And it worked. As I would come to learn, time and time again, there are many different methods of finding a way to believe. This was just one.

~~~

IN MANY WAYS, I saved the best for last with this chapter. Not to put too fine a point on it, but belief is everything.

That's not to say everything else is unimportant. On the contrary, when struggling with hardship, we need to be aware of these other dimensions to truly understand that belief rests on a different plane and is powerful beyond our understanding.

During the darkest times of both of my big struggles, I have tried many ways to push myself to believe. I found my attempts circle around a few main categories. I call these the Brands of Belief:

- **Seeing:** Seeing someone who has gone before and found a successful outcome.

- **Absorbing:** Leveraging inspirational content, be it in quotes, books, or music.

- **Asking and Receiving:** Asking the people closest to you to help you believe in yourself.

- **Doing:** Pushing yourself to explore the limits of what you can do.

- **Trusting:** Having faith things will work out.

SEEING

I have referenced this path previously when discussing people like Amy Purdy or my lung transplant rehab friend Charlie. My favorite part of this brand of belief is it lets your mind and heart fast-forward the movie of your life to the happy ending. Seeing there can be a positive outcome can be so incredibly inspiring when you're still living amid the rubble of the initial shock of the situation.

In the weeks before my lung transplant, at a check-up appointment I told the team that I had been feeling better and requiring less oxygen. Even this single hopeful comment led to the medical team doubling down on ensuring I understood my current state was a very temporary Band-Aid and that my heart (because of my lung pressure) remained in major distress. In the appointment that day, I was warned it wouldn't be completely out of the norm for me to drop dead at any time. I'm sure the words they used were more eloquent, but that was what I heard. It was a cold-water plunge if I ever experienced one.

So, needless to say, meeting someone with a positive outcome that week was a gift of belief I desperately needed. I was walking into a waiting area to get bloodwork and X-rays done, and an older gentleman came up to me completely unprompted. Maybe it was because I had my green oxygen tank with me. Maybe it was divine intervention. This was not a transplant area of the hospital; I was in the general lab area where everyone gets blood drawn and basic X-rays.

Out of the blue he said to me, "Hey, I just had a lung transplant nine months ago and I'm doing awesome!"

I started to tear up and gave him the headlines of my situation. As he and his wife walked away, he said, "I don't know why I came and talked to you. Maybe God just told me to." It was the best belief medicine. I didn't ask his name in my blissful confusion, but I have referred to him ever since as "Clarence."

Sharing stories of success—even a quick note in a text, such as, "My nephew had a double lung transplant ten years ago and climbed mountains in Colorado the year after his surgery"—is a huge gift to those you care about.

This brand of belief can also be gained by just catching a glimpse of the good stuff around the corner, even if it's not the full movie.

My dad had a major stroke at 63 years old, which was just a few years after my accident. He was always fit and active, so we were all shocked. Coming on the heels of an abdominal surgery, he was suddenly unable to walk, talk, or do much of anything. Things were not looking good. Contrary to his naturally optimistic and selfless nature, it seemed he was giving up. He would fight against eating and going to therapy. We didn't know what to do.

My mom, my sister, and I would take turns caring for him in the hospital. One evening I took him on a walk in a wheelchair, which felt like a bit of a role reversal, me being the one pushing the wheelchair. I could tell he did enjoy going on walks, though he couldn't communicate verbally at this point. Unbeknownst to me, it was forbidden to take him off the hospital campus without permission (we did get in trouble!), but I didn't think about it as we were simply going on a walk. It was a gorgeous summer evening, and we stopped for a rest at the apartment complex where my mom was staying (thanks to a friend who shared her condo with us). The complex has a beautiful hilltop vista, and my dad was just taking it all in. I'm sure this was an even more stunning view after so many days inside hospital walls. Suddenly, he got this determined look in his eyes and tried to stand up. I helped him a little, and he stood up and breathed in the fresh air and inspiring view. He tilted his head up to the sky and held out his arms a little, at least the side that still had mobility. From that night on, he started to fully participate in therapy. He became a fierce rehab warrior and regained much of his function. We got so much of our amazing dad back.

A glimpse of the outside world and an inspiring sunset and fresh air allowed him to believe. He got to see what could be, and that's exactly what he needed.

Hospital walls, despite the caring people inside them, can drain your belief coffers. I can totally relate. Years after I took my dad on that walk, he did the same for me (along with my mom). They took me on my first trip outside of the hospital room after my lung surgery, when I was feeling beyond stir-crazy because I hadn't been allowed to leave. Simply having a new view—it was a big window, looking out at the rain—completely changed my outlook that day. Seeing to believing. It's huge.

ABSORBING

Some people really find value in taking in inspiring content. I'm one of those people. You may be too, since you are taking the time to read this book.

During my winter of depression following the amputation and other limb issues, I sought out a counselor. I was in a terrible mindset and needed something to help me crawl out of the hole. Counseling, it should be noted, doesn't generally provide a light-switch moment, but it, along with some of the other tactics in this book, were a great help in my journey back to positivity.

A very simple yet effective tool I remember from one of those first counseling sessions was a box of quotes. The counselor told me to take the quotes home and select the five that spoke to me the most. This exercise helped me to understand and articulate what I was feeling in the moment and provided direction for where I wanted to be, as well as adding some hope to my soul. Thinking back, I can only recall one of the five quotes I selected, as it was one that has helped drive me forward on many days:

"The only way out is through." ROBERT FROST

What I adore about this quote is the power packed into its simplicity. It says to me:

- You have to keep going; there is no alternative.

- You must feel the pain, do the work, and walk the path; there are no shortcuts.

- You can get out of this hard place. There is an open field on the other side of the dense forest you find yourself in, and it will be glorious when you arrive.

Here's an interesting tidbit. In the course of writing this book, I learned that the quote above, attributed to Robert Frost, is actually a little different. In his poem "A Servant to Servants," from his 1914 book *North of Boston*, the direct quote is "The best way out is always through." The difference is subtle but huge at the same time. The actual quote tells us there is another way out; you can make the choice not to go through. In my reading and from my experience, this other way is the path of despair and bitterness. Of giving in. No matter which quote you use for inspiration, it seems to me that for our health and happiness, we must always choose to go *through*.

If you have a friend who is struggling, send them a screen grab of a quote (or recommend a book)—that might be all the words of encouragement they need to help get them through. A few friends of mine were especially good at sending the right words at just the right time. I discovered my thoughtful daughter has a towering strength in this practice, delivered in her homemade signs and cards.

Music is another absorbing method I find especially helpful, as it blends inspiring words with the power to lift your soul in the way only music can do. Music can be very personal, so it is sometimes harder to share, but give it a shot. You might create an earworm for a person in need who will cling to it when it seems there's not much else to hold on to.

When you're not fighting desperately to find hope, you might think quotes, books, or songs are not that big a deal. But I'm telling you, every little ounce of inspiration matters when you feel you are hanging by a thread.

〜〜

WHEN DEALING WITH trauma and kids, this method of absorbing belief is immeasurably helpful, particularly when it comes to movies and storybooks. When I became an amputee, my kids were two and four, so the simplicity of the messages found in these mediums was perfect for them to find something positive to latch on to.

We found the movie *Dolphin Tale* more helpful than anything else. This film features the true story of Winter the dolphin, who was injured and needed a prosthetic tail. Amid an entertaining storyline is the demonstration of how a prosthetic works and how Winter was eventually able to function well again. When I was healed and walking well again, we went to visit Winter in person at the Clearwater Marine Aquarium where she lived.

We also received a book from my wonderful cousins called *Molly the Pony*. It is also a true story about an animal that needs a prosthetic. Molly was abandoned in Hurricane Katrina and then rescued. She was attacked by a dog on the farm where she went after the hurricane and needed an amputation to save her life. The book does a great job of explaining what an amputation is and how Molly adapted.

Finally, I'd be remiss if I didn't mention my friend Patrick, who wrote a children's book called *Mr. Bear's Big Dream: Overcoming Life's Challenges Through Determination and Perseverance*. I'm a little biased as he thoughtfully dedicated this project to me, but regardless, it's an adorable book that highlights how you can overcome any challenge.

ASKING AND RECEIVING

"Do you think I'm going to die?" This is the question I asked on repeat the day of the boating accident. I wanted those around me to tell me I wasn't going to die because I was so petrified. That's asking for belief from others.

"Do you think I can really do this?" This is the question I asked my inner circle, especially my parents and sister, when I was learning to walk again. Asking for their belief in me.

"Mom, you are walking so fast today." That's my then four-year-old son on a walk with me and my newish prosthetic. Receiving belief—thanks to his initiative and kindness.

It's 100 percent okay to ask people to help you believe in yourself in whatever way you want to ask the question. It's important to note, though, that the replies that break through are always spoken with a genuine belief on the giver's side. Otherwise, they are just empty words. Seeking out these conversations can be helpful and necessary when you don't have any fortitude in the moment to believe in yourself.

DOING

The Mexico zip-lining story is a perfect example of this brand of belief.

You simply must get up and do! Recall Martin Luther King Jr.'s sage words: "If you cannot run, walk."

No matter the hardship, there is always something to do— something to push. It might be as simple as rolling over in bed or as difficult as crawling up stairs. But no matter the result, it is the effort of doing that matters. By doing, you are making an active choice to believe.

In the hospital after my lung transplant, there was a lot of doing to be done. Though not fun, it did have the benefit of creating belief. The two physical requirements to get out of the hospital were to be able to walk 1,000 steps without stopping and to walk for 30 minutes on a treadmill at any speed.

The first day I was out of the intensive care unit, a physical therapist came into my room and said we were going to work on the 1,000-step goal. At this point I was still in the hospital granny gown with the open back end. I was hooked up to many devices, including drainage tubes in my chest. But off we went with a nurse pushing IV poles and holding my drainage boxes. I was amazed at how great I felt, considering I had still been intubated 48 hours before and had slept terribly for days.

The therapist told me there wasn't a goal for day one; she simply suggested I should walk until I couldn't. So, I kept walking and walking, not having any context for how far 1,000 steps was in the hospital setting. Next thing you know, all the nurses and staff members started watching and cheering me on. We rounded a corner and the therapist said, "You did your 1,000 steps! Ring the gong!" I didn't even know there was a gong.

Somehow, I had achieved the goal on my very first attempt. After the crustiest days imaginable in the ICU, reaching this goal made me believe in the most fantastical of futures. And the gong was a nice touch.

For those of you who are caregivers, parents, or managers at work, part of your responsibility is to let others explore ways to find belief in themselves. Let them have a reasonable amount of space to stretch outside of their comfort zone to experience the belief that comes from doing something they didn't think they could do.

TRUSTING

For me, this one is all about my relationship with God. For you it might be Allah, or Buddha, or the divine spirits of the universe, or wherever your belief system aligns. No matter the case, I believe it is crucial to have a relationship with something larger than yourself. Doing so is the only way you can unlock the truly divine brand of belief found in trust.

After all I went through during the initial year of getting to—and having—the lung transplant, I would be remiss to not include how my trust in God was by far the biggest factor in my being able to move forward.

I have always, to some degree, been a person of faith. There are many scriptures in the Bible that talk about the purpose of hardship and suffering. I feel like I have a much better grasp on those words now, as this extreme set of circumstances drew me closer to God than I had ever been. The result was a peace that I cannot adequately describe; it defies logic. It's about trust, and it's beautiful when you feel it. And it's available to all of us.

The Bible says in Hebrews 11:1 (NIV), "Now faith is the assurance of things hoped for, the conviction of things not seen." And in Proverbs 3:5 (NIV), "Trust in the Lord with all your heart and lean not on your own understanding."

I used those general concepts many times in my own spiritual growth. It boiled down to this for me:

- **I don't know what will happen in my life**. None of us does. If I only use my own human logic and the stats and odds of my situation, I will never stop thinking and worrying.

- **I, do, however, trust that God will take care of things**, including things I don't yet completely understand.

Let me tell you this wasn't and isn't just blind faith. When I opened myself up to this kind of thinking, I experienced many examples of godly assurance.

For instance, when I was in the hospital for the first time after my lung condition was diagnosed, I was alone at night and struggling to shut off my worries and sleep. I couldn't believe that here I was spending nights in the hospital again. Suffering in sorrow, I suddenly heard in my head, over and over again, the lyrics "a little messed up, but we're all alright," which is from a Kenny Chesney song called "American Kids." Over the course of the coming months, that song would come to me in the strangest and most necessary of times. It was like God was talking to me and telling me things were going to be okay, no matter how bleak my circumstances. It was uncanny how those lyrics would pop into my head when I needed comfort most. From 50-plus nights in hospital rooms, to moments when I didn't think I could breathe, to the aftermath of scary appointments or test results, there were lots of times when I needed reassurance.

Another way I trusted in God was when I asked Him to help me decide where to do the full transplant evaluation. As I've noted, it wasn't possible to get the transplant in Kansas City, so we had to explore other options.

Different doctors recommended different hospitals for different reasons, so we had a lot to consider. In partnership with our Kansas City health care team, we narrowed it down to two great hospitals. One was in Dallas and the other in St. Louis.

I was torn and kept weighing the pros and cons as well as concerns about getting accepted. The underlying condition I have is a tricky one, so not all transplant programs are willing to take cases like mine.

I had prayed my whole life, but I hadn't really asked for guidance in this way before. I decided to give it a try because I was desperate for help with this life-defining decision. They say God works in mysterious ways, and it wasn't until a couple of days later, while driving to meet my family at my son's baseball game, that I earnestly asked again for guidance. Literally the second after I completed the thought, I noticed the road sign right above me. It only said, "St. Louis." I'm sure I'd seen that sign before—I mean, I've driven this stretch of road many times—but that's not the point. The timing of my ability to *see* the sign—the sign God was giving me—was crazy. Frankly, it is hard to explain how vivid this moment was for me. Logically, you might be tempted to say that it was simply a coincidence. But this is the key factor in the trusting step: you must give yourself over, completely, and be open to all possibilities. I also feel like it's a "when you know, you know" type of feeling. God's sign to me gave me confidence in choosing St. Louis, despite some concern I wouldn't be accepted. And thankfully, they accepted me into their program, and it was a perfect choice for me and our family. The entire transplant team was incredible and the proximity to home made the process much easier than if we had chosen Dallas, which was twice as far away. I am beyond grateful I ended up in St. Louis.

This growing belief and trust helped me navigate things I couldn't have navigated on my own. I received a transplant call just four days after going on the transplant list, just as we were driving home from St. Louis after my evaluation. We couldn't believe the call came so soon, and we were equal parts thrilled and petrified.

After a night in the hospital (again), arranging for my kids to be driven the four hours to St. Louis to see me (as I hadn't yet been home after the pre-transplant evaluation), and doing all of the pre-op rigamarole, I was told, "We actually aren't going to be able to do surgery today."

This is what they call a "dry run," meaning you get all the way to the pre-operating stage before you discover the potential new lungs are not viable. It's like you're at the five-yard line and going for the touchdown with only seconds left on the clock when all of a sudden the game ends prematurely.

If not for my trust in God, this would have been devastating. The medical team was very pensive when reporting the news to me. It didn't faze me one bit. My initial thought was, *This wasn't meant to be. Something else will work out as it should.* Trust. It's freeing. It creates a peace like no other. And I continue to believe I'm a little messed up but I'm all right.

I've met many other medical unicorns along the paths I have walked. I can't think of a single one of them who didn't have some sort of faith that helped get them through their challenges. Obviously, faith is personal, so it shows up differently for different people. However, the idea is universal and unifying.

The last thing I'll offer up is this:

I've tried it both ways. I relied on my faith during my leg journey, but it was more garden-variety faith—even though I didn't understand that at the time. With my leg, I relied more on my own grit and the other brands of belief above. I made it through, but it was hard. I was angry and depressed, and I felt terribly alone many times. During my lung journey, however, faith and trust were paramount, and through them I found hope and belief. And while I may have felt angry or depressed at times, I never felt alone. And that, in and of itself, is all the reward I needed to believe in trusting.

"Faith is to believe what you do not see; the reward of this faith is to see what you believe." SAINT AUGUSTINE

~~~

WHEN IT BECAME CLEAR I was going to need a lung transplant, I was so anxious. Couple that with the daily struggles of not being able to breathe, and it was hard to keep moving forward with any sort of positive spirit. I distinctly remember one spring Saturday afternoon sitting in my car in between my daughter's softball games. I was desperate for someone to reassure me things would be okay, but the reality was no one in my circle had ever had a lung transplant, so no one could truly know what was ahead for me.

So, I texted the one person I "knew" who had been down this road. His name was Bob, and he was a friend of a friend. He had been diagnosed with the same scleroderma and pulmonary hypertension I had, and through a former colleague of mine we connected.

My message that day to "Bob Lung Friend," as he was then labeled in my phone, was that it was looking very likely I was going to need a lung transplant. I asked him for "any nuggets of optimism or inspiration to send my way." Clearly, I was desperate for someone with credibility in this space to help calm my nerves.

When Bob's response popped up on my screen, I scrambled to read it like I had found water in the desert. But his response was not what I wanted to hear. Instead of telling me it was all going to be okay, he acknowledged the path would be difficult. His main message was to "give it to God." Essentially, something like this is too overwhelming to take on alone. Relieve the burden by letting God and the doctor's advice guide me.

After the first few minutes of feeling frustrated that I hadn't received the reassuring words I was desperate to hear, I let his wise and eloquent message sink in. I had already been quite faithful during the previous months of hardship, but this notion of "giving it to God" wasn't something I had actively tried to do before. Many of us have heard that phrase; it's thrown out like a platitude. "Give it to God." I had never actually tried to do so in a meaningful way. In that moment, I decided I would try.

By this time, I was sitting in my lawn chair waiting on my daughter's game to start. The sky was a hazy pink and blue that day. I distinctly recall its soothing presence as I silently asked God, while looking up at that calm sky, to help me learn how to give Him this challenge. That was phase one of my learning journey to do the thing we easily say, "give it to God."

Just two days later I had one of the most intense medical tests I've ever endured, and that's saying something. I honestly don't even remember what the test was aiming to discover, but I do remember how horrible it was.

It was an MRI with a twist. In addition to going into the claustrophobic MRI tube, I had to do several breathing exercises in the tube. I was still on the 24-7 medicine pump, so we had to have that thing all juiced and ready to go for the duration of the test and find a place to nestle it in around the MRI straitjacket confinement. I couldn't breathe without oxygen by this time, especially not lying flat, so add to the discomfort the oxygen cannula in my nostrils (the urge to scratch an itch when your hands are tied up is tenfold when you have oxygen in your nose!). And I also had to remove my prosthetic leg for the procedure—more fun!

Once in the MRI tube, I had to take deep breaths and hold them. It was agony. I bet I had to do 60 of these, and if I didn't hold my breath long enough, I had to start over. This process took an excruciating 46 minutes. The entire time I felt like I couldn't hold my breath one second longer, and the mental torture of doing all of this in that claustrophobic tube was almost more than I could handle.

When I was let out of the tube and sent on my merry way, I was exhausted and a bit traumatized. Driving home, I wasn't reflecting on Bob's advice to give it to God; I was simply in a mental daze. I decided to call Granny as I drove home. She was nearing her final days, so I tried to give her a call when I could. I'm surprised in hindsight I did so on this day, considering my mental state. Maybe it was divine intervention again. Depending on the day during this time of her life, Granny's lucidity could vary. She was always very sharp with her long-term memory, as is common for older people, but other aspects of conversation would vary from call to call.

I hadn't told her—nor had anyone else—about my latest medical challenges because I didn't want her to worry. However, I was hungry for her wisdom. During the call that day, I generalized my question to try and get that wisdom without having to disclose all the details. I said something like, "I know you've faced a lot of medical challenges in your life. How did you get through it all?" I assumed she would think I was referring to my life as an amputee.

I'll never forget her words. She was so lucid, clear, and wise. She simply said, "I learned to give it to God. It's a lot easier that way." The timing was uncanny. I had challenged myself to do exactly that just 48 hours before, thanks to Bob's nudge. And I love how she mentioned, "it's easier that way." I have found so much wisdom in that statement.

Granny had dealt with a hysterectomy (which was no small thing in the 1960s), thyroid removal, colon cancer, lymphoma, skin cancer, and a host of other medical issues over the course of her 89 years. Unprompted, her next words to me were, "I used to pray I would be around to raise my daughters, and here I am with great-grandchildren." Those words wrapped a blanket around my heart. When I read all the terrifying risks and warnings that came with my condition, it was impossible to not harbor major concerns about possibly not being there for my children. The here and now. Graduations. College moms' weekends. First jobs.

Weddings. Babies. To hear her say exactly what I needed to hear in the calmest and clearest voice was such a blessing to me.

Calling her that day didn't feel like happenstance. Catching her with the highest mental clarity and brightest of moods. Extracting her deep wisdom. Hearing the same thing Bob had just said and that I had challenged myself to do. Give it to God.

Over the following weeks and months, I tried hard to do just that. When I got scared or overwhelmed, I would remind myself the situation was beyond my control and to let God handle it. I would pray for my faith and skill at actually letting go to be strengthened. Miraculously, I felt a perfect peace beyond understanding during this process. The circumstances were so dark, and the daily challenges were so frustrating, that it didn't make sense that I would feel at peace and even joyful at times. I worried if I shared the details of my circumstance on one hand and how I felt on the other, people would think I was sugar-coating it. But I wasn't. The better I got at letting go, the better I felt.

I truly felt the peace you read about, that goes beyond logic and our own understanding.

WRAP-UP

It's essential to find a way to believe that you can overcome. If you can't see it and can't feel it, it will be hard to do it. There are so many ways to find those fragments of hope, but it takes conscious effort to look for them when it feels like all hope is lost. The good news: the struggle gets a lot easier when you do find a way to believe. Believing things just might work out is the best perspective of all.

Epilogue

OVER THE COURSE of writing my TEDx Talk, then writing this book, I figured I'd encountered the most daunting aspects of writing—that is, until I sat down to write a letter to my anonymous organ donor's family. I only knew two things: first, my organ donor was a 39-year-old man and, second, I didn't have the words to adequately express my gratitude. But I had to try, right?

I sent a card, and in it I tried as best I could to offer my sincere gratitude and deep thanks while also acknowledging that the gift I was given meant they had suffered a tremendous loss. Someday I hope to learn more about my donor, but for now I'll take solace in the fact that his family knows how much his choice—and their resulting actions—mattered.

Because of him and his family, I have received a miracle. To be able to breathe again and let my heart heal (literally and figuratively) is a gift beyond comprehension. Organ donation is a selfless act that impacts lives in gigantic ways.

Sometimes I think about the breathtaking fact that I am walking around with a part of someone else inside of me. His story is now a part of my story, and his precious lungs let me:

breathe

walk

talk

laugh

pray

sing

live.

In a way, we are all walking around with parts of others inside of us. When people tell their stories, little bits of them stay with us forever.

Life gives us all gifts, sometimes delivered with big red bows and sometimes in less obvious wrapping. Sometimes we don't even recognize something is a gift until we open it, study it, and sit with it awhile. And, quite frankly, it may not look like a gift to anyone else who hasn't examined it. But it's what we do with that gift—how we choose to share it—that really matters.

A life of big red bows may seem ideal, but that's not how life works, even if we wanted it to. The real art of living, in my humble opinion, is how you navigate those unexpected deliveries.

"Life is not always a matter of holding good cards,
but sometimes, playing a poor hand well." JOSH BILLINGS

Acknowledgments

There are so many people to thank, both in the journey of writing this book and in the journey of my life that ultimately shaped these stories. I'm sure I'll accidentally leave someone out or mess something up, but cue vulnerability—I'm going to give this a shot.

I will start by thanking God for caring for me in every moment included in these stories. He has a unique plan for my life, and I am humbled every day to try and live out what I am supposed to do to serve my purpose. Sometimes I feel like I'm getting it right, sometimes I feel like I'm falling short, but I will keep moving forward trying to live this path carved out for me. Like I said in the chapter on belief, because of God I have never been alone despite the most isolating of circumstances.

Aaron. He's the one who has lived all this hardship—and joy—right alongside me. His (giant, size 15) footsteps are always found right ahead of me to clear the way, right behind me to make sure I don't fall, or right beside me when times are good. I have leaned on his capable shoulders many times, including literally when walking down public staircases to keep my balance and avoid the germ-ridden handrails. His parents knew what they were doing when they named him, because the name Aaron means "mountain of strength." I'm so glad we met that night at the Royals game in parking lot J, where I spent a lot of my childhood.

To my kids, Mitchell and Morgan. Their footprints are also all over so many of these memories and triumphs. They have saved me time and again, even though they may not know it. It's because of them I got out from under the boat. It's because of them I got out of bed many a morning. It's because of them I fought so hard. It's because of them I get to experience the best parts of the life I have clawed to keep. I hope they choose to share their gifts with the world, because they have so many.

To my mom and dad. They are truly models of unconditional love. I have always been supported, cheered for, and taken care of, and that is the gift of a lifetime. Plus, these two taught me how to have fun! Whenever I call, it is always a "yes," no matter the ask.

Angela (Rara, Ang). When you are on the struggle bus for so long, you have to have people to lean on, and it can't always be your significant other because they are deep in the trauma with you. My sister was that person for me. I called and FaceTimed and texted her so many times, including during many all-out panics about whatever the situation was that day. I would let my guard down with her, and she would drop everything for me. Somehow, she always found a way to calm my nerves. Plus, after she swooped in, my house never looked so clean.

Vicky, my mother-in-law slash second mom. She spent countless days with us during both medical dramas. She would quietly move in to the guest room and just fill in all the holes and do all the work. She's also a really good listener, and I'm grateful for our frequent texting sessions at midnight when normal-houred people are already sleeping.

To our many wonderful friends and family. Those who checked on me. Spent time taking care of me. Prayed for us. Made us laugh. Took care of our kids. Helped in countless ways, both functionally and emotionally. Thank you.

To the residents of Clyde, Kansas; Howells, Nebraska; and Basehor, Kansas. Small-town people have my heart.

Those featured in this book. Thank you for being willing to share your stories and insights with me and with the world. Mick, Billy, Shirene, Charlie, Kelly, Luis, Hannah, Tiffany, Holly, Bob, and Dad—thank you for your courage and vulnerability.

The giant medical community in my world. My doctors, nurses, prosthetic team, pharmacists, and many more, I am grateful for each of you. I have the best team imaginable.

To my Hallmark family. Thank you for supporting me and caring for me in all the ways. You guys really are *the very best*.

Steve, my editor. You won't want me to include you in this, but I'm not letting you edit this out. I pontificated for years about writing a book but could never get off the dime. Then one day you emailed me. Though I had talked to other publishing professionals, you helped me shape my concept for this book in our first discussion. The care and expertise you've given this project made it exponentially better.

To my organ donor and family. I still don't have adequate words to express my gratitude. I hope I am living my life in a way that honors the gift you gave me.

Notes

The following is a quick guide for those who wish to follow up on a fact or to read more about the topics discussed. Quotes from interviews I conducted and conversations I had, and the like, are not cited here.

INTRODUCTION

"This well-known phenomenon is how our brains work . . ."
> Valtteri Arstila, "Time Slows Down During Accidents," *Frontiers in Psychology* 27, no. 3 (June 2012), https://doi.org/10.3389/fpsyg.2012.00196.

CHAPTER 1: CHOOSE YOUR VIEW

"Studies have proven that the psychological phenomenon behind perspective shifting, positive thinking, not only shifts your emotional state but also leads to better health . . ."
> "The Power of Positive Thinking," Johns Hopkins Medicine, November 1, 2021, https://www.hopkinsmedicine.org/health/wellness-and-prevention/the-power-of-positive-thinking.

"The couple months that followed [my hospital admission] were a blur . . ."
> Shirene Philipose, "Taking Off the White Coat, Putting on the Hospital Gown: A Resident's Perspective on Being a Patient," *Human Factor, UMKC Medicine* (2023): 14.

"Martine is currently spearheading research and solutions for lung transplants."
> Adam Piore, "Pharma CEO Faces Personal Fight for a New Breed of Organ Donors," *Bloomberg Businessweek*, July 30, 2021, https://www.bloomberg.com/news/features/2021-07-30/pharma-ceo-rothblatt-faces-personal-fight-for-new-breed-of-organ-donors.

CHAPTER 2: OPEN UP

"Within a year, this campaign, and others like it, nearly doubled the profits of the company."
> Kiley Skene, "A PR Case Study: Dove Real Beauty Campaign," *News Generation*, April 11, 2014, https://newsgeneration.com/2014/04/11/pr-case-study-dove-real-beauty.

"Brené Brown says, 'we don't have to do all of it alone' . . ."
> Brené Brown, *Rising Strong: How the Ability to Reset Transforms the Way We Live, Love, Parent, and Lead* (New York: Random House, 2017), 177.

"I believe that you have to walk through vulnerability . . ."
> "About Brené," Brené Brown website, https://brenebrown.com/about.

"Her 2012 book, *Daring Greatly*, starts with an excerpt . . ."
> Theodore Roosevelt, "Citizenship in a Republic," speech at the Sorbonne, Paris, April 23, 1910, quoted in Brené Brown, *Daring Greatly: How the Courage to Be Vulnerable Transforms the Way We Live, Love, Parent, and Lead* (New York: Gotham, 2012), 1.

"It was in 2012, just before she published *Daring Greatly*."
> Brené Brown, *Dare to Lead: Brave Work. Tough Conversations. Whole Hearts.* (New York: Random House, 2018), xviii.

"In September 2021, the *Wall Street Journal* obtained internal Facebook documents . . ."
> "Facebook's Documents About Instagram and Teens, Published," *Wall Street Journal*, September 29, 2021, https://www.wsj.com/articles/facebook-documents-instagram-teens-11632953840.

CHAPTER 3: REFRAME

"The Tim McGraw song 'Live Like You Were Dying' hits differently now."

Tim Nichols and Craig Wiseman, "Live Like You Were Dying," sung by Tim McGraw (Big Loud Publishing, 2004).

"As Annie Gowen reported in the *Washington Post* . . ."

Annie Gowen, "The Town That Built Back Green," *Washington Post*, October 23, 2020, https://www.washingtonpost.com/climate-solutions/2020/10/22/greensburg-kansas-wind-power-carbon-emissions/.

"As entrepreneur and philanthropist Richard Branson said . . ."

"12 Famous People Who Struggled with Dyslexia Before Changing the World," *ISME Journal*, November 21, 2017, https://journal.imse.com/12-famous-people-who-struggled-with-dyslexia-before-changing-the-world/.

CHAPTER 4: DIG DEEP

"Most of the important things in the world have been accomplished by people . . ."

Dale Carnegie, *Dale Carnegie's Scrapbook: A Treasury of the Wisdom of the Ages*, ed. Dorothy Carnegie (New York: Dale Carnegie & Associates, 1959), 199.

"It's not that I'm so smart . . ."

James P. Gray, "It's a Gray Area: Einstein's Brilliant Thoughts Pertinent to Today's Woes," *Los Angeles Times*, May 31, 2013, https://www.latimes.com/socal/daily-pilot/opinion/tn-dpt-me-0602-gray-20130531-story.html.

"Start where you are. Use what you have. Do what you can."

"Quotes by Arthur Ashe," Arthur Ashe website, accessed March 30, 2023, http://www.cmgww.com/sports/ashe/quotes/.

CHAPTER 5: CHECK YOURSELF

"Don't spend a lot of time imagining the worst-case scenario."

Michael J. Fox, *A Funny Thing Happened on the Way to the Future . . . Twists and Turns and Lessons Learned* (New York: Hachette Books, 2010).

"Assumptions are at the heart of many miscommunications."

"Assumptions Lead to Miscommunication," *Medical Xpress*, February 23, 2007, https://medicalxpress.com/news/2007-02-assumptions-miscommunication.html.

"You can't just visualize it and go eat a sandwich."

"What Oprah Learned from Jim Carrey," Oprah.com, October 12, 2011, https://www.oprah.com/oprahs-lifeclass/what-oprah-learned-from-jim-carrey-video.

"Visualization has been proven to increase . . ."

Vinoth K. Ranganathan et al., "From Mental Power to Muscle Power—Gaining Strength by Using the Mind," *Neuropsychologia* 42, no. 7 (2004): 944–56, https://doi.org/10.1016/j.neuropsychologia.2003.11.018.

Thomas Newmark, "Cases in Visualization for Improved Athletic Performance," *Psychiatric Annals* 42, no. 10 (2012): 385–87, https://doi.org/10.3928/00485713-20121003-07.

Nicolò F. Bernardi et al., "Mental Practice Promotes Motor Anticipation: Evidence from Skilled Music Performance," *Frontiers in Human Neuroscience* 20, no. 7 (2013), https://doi.org/10.3389/fnhum.2013.00451.

Yannis Theodorakis et al., "The Effect of Self-Talk on Injury Rehabilitation," *European Yearbook of Sport Psychology* 2 (1998): 124–35.

Antonis Hatzigeorgiadis et al., "Mechanisms Underlying the Self-Talk–Performance Relationship: The Effects of Motivational Self-Talk on Self-Confidence and Anxiety,"

Psychology of Sport and Exercise 10, no. 1 (January 2009): 186–92, https://doi.org/10.1016/j.psychsport.2008.07.009.

"Plant your goal in your mind . . ."

Earl Nightingale, *The Strangest Secret* (Melrose, FL: Laurenzana Press at Smashwords, 2011).

"What is the use of living . . ."

Winston Churchill, speech at Dundee, Scotland, October 10, 1908, https://winstonchurchill.org/resources/quotes/quotes-falsely-attributed/#:~:text=What%20You%20Get-,'You%20make%20a%20living%20by%20what%20you%20get%3B%20you%20make,spoke%20or%20wrote%20those%20words.

CHAPTER 6: BE A RISER

"If you can't fly then run . . ."

Martin Luther King Jr., speech, YouTube, accessed March 30, 2023, https://www.youtube.com/watch?v=MFOFS0iAwDg

"The notion of rising was captured beautifully in a song . . ."

Travis Meadows and Steve Moakler, "Riser," sung by Dierks Bentley (Capitol Records Nashville, 2014).

"Think of a packet of seeds . . ."

David Goggins, *Never Finished: Unshackle Your Mind and Win the War Within* (Austin, TX: Lioncrest, 2022).

"The knowledge that you have emerged wiser and stronger . . ."

J.K. Rowling, Harvard commencement address, June 5, 2008, https://www.jkrowling.com/harvard-commencement-address/.

"All the adversity I've had in my life . . ."

Lewis Howes, "20 Lessons from Walt Disney on Entrepreneurship, Innovation and Chasing Your Dreams," *Forbes*, July 17, 2012, https://www.forbes.com/sites/lewishowes/2012/07/17/20-business-quotes-and-lessons-from-walt-disney/.

"This poem, in its entirety, is the stuff of resilience."

Dr. Oliver Tearle, "'I Am the Master of My Fate': A Short Analysis of William Ernest Henley's 'Invictus,'" Interesting Literature, February 2017, https://interestingliterature.com/2017/02/i-am-the-master-of-my-fate-a-short-analysis-of-william-ernest-henleys-invictus/.

CHAPTER 7: ENGAGE YOUR SOUL

"If I have the belief that I can do it . . ."

Ashoka, "12 Great Quotes from Gandhi on His Birthday," *Forbes*, October 2, 2012, https://www.forbes.com/sites/ashoka/2012/10/02/12-great-quotes-from-gandhi-on-his-birthday/?sh=72a4be5933d8.

"The best way out is always through."

Robert Frost, *North of Boston* (New York: Henry Holt, 1914), 66.

"I suddenly heard in my head, over and over again, the lyrics 'a little messed up, but we're all alright'. . ."

Rodney Clawson, Luke Laird, and Shane McAnally, "American Kids," sung by Kenny Chesney (Blue Chair, 2014).

EPILOGUE

"Life is not always a matter of holding good cards . . ."

Josh Billings, *Josh Billings on Ice, and Other Things* (New York: G.W. Carleton, 1870), 89.

About the Author

LINDSEY ROY has twice needed surgery to save her life. First, a leg amputation after a traumatic boating accident and then, a double lung transplant after being diagnosed with a rare and progressive disease that constricted the blood vessels in her lungs. These experiences, coupled with her natural gifts for speaking and writing, have created a passion in Lindsey to tell her story in the hopes of helping others tackle whatever obstacles life throws at them. Her 2017 TEDx Talk, "What Trauma Taught Me About Happiness," has been viewed by nearly 200,000 people. Her story has been featured in major publications, such as *O Magazine*, *Fast Company*, *Forbes*, and *Working Mother*.

Lindsey's perspective is sharpened by her roles as a corporate executive, mother, and wife. She is Senior VP of Strategy & Brand at Hallmark Cards, where she has worked for more than 20 years and has led various initiatives and groups—many of which call upon the lessons shared in *The Gift of Perspective*. She has a degree in Journalism & Advertising with a minor in Speech from Kansas State University and serves on charitable boards, including Ability KC and Steps of Faith Foundation, an organization that provides prosthetics to the uninsured and underinsured. Her greatest joy in life is spending time with her family—her husband, Aaron, and children, Mitchell and Morgan. This is Lindsey's first book.